Winterflight

Other books by Joseph Bayly

The Gospel Blimp
Congo Crisis
The Last Thing We Talk About
Out of My Mind
Heaven
I Love to Tell the Story
What about Horoscopes?
Psalms of My Life
I Saw Gooley Fly

Winterflight

a novel by
JOSEPH BAYLY

WORD BOOKS
PUBLISHER
WACO, TEXAS

ISBN 0–8499–0297–5
Library of Congress catalog card number: 81–51006
Printed in the United States of America

To Our Children
Friends and Critics

TREES LINED both sides of Auden Drive in Wayne, Pennsylvania, touching each other, mingling their branches across the quiet street. They were maples, planted to celebrate the nation's bicentennial more than thirty years before.

It was a Tuesday morning in early September, a month that can be exceptionally hot in Philadelphia and its suburbs, when steamy air arises from the Delaware and Schuylkill rivers, blanketing a wide area.

Halfway down the street was a modest house with a carefully kept lawn. A child's bicycle leaned against the house's side, near a rose garden enclosed by a low white fence.

Inside the house, two people sat at a breakfast table. The woman spoke. "For six years I've worried about this day coming, but then I'd pray about it and hope it never would. And now to have it happen at the beginning of school. Maybe we shouldn't have gotten him the bike."

Grace Stanton had beautiful eyes, eyes that revealed the integrity of her thirty-six years, eyes that were blue like the ocean she loved. Now her eyes were frightened, as if she were looking at something and was afraid of what she saw.

Her husband answered, "Why cry about water that's over the

dam? We can't change things now, even if we were wrong. And anyway, we decided at the very start that we'd let him have a normal childhood. So we didn't alarm him. I guess we set ourselves up for something like this."

Jonathan Stanton sat opposite his wife at the small table. He finished eating and moved the dish to the side, placing a steaming cup of coffee in its place. He was a big man but carried no extra weight. His eyes were harder to read than his wife's, but now they showed a kindred worry. He had the junior executive's bearing and displayed his impatience. He was a year older than Grace.

"Maybe we did set ourselves up for it," Grace said, "but it was that fall he had off the bike. If it hadn't been for that—"

"It was bound to be something. He could just as easily have fallen down the stairs, or running at school. And you've done a great job of getting him to come to you for ice and the pressure bandage whenever he's hurt. Which hasn't been often. By the way, is he awake yet?"

Stephen was a bright, affectionate boy, in first grade at school—and he was a mild hemophiliac. In his six years, he had not had a really serious bleeding incident, just a series of minor injuries. But now he had fallen off his bicycle and bruised his hip.

"No, he was still sleeping when I came downstairs. If he had only come right away this time. Oh, I wish we hadn't gotten him that bike." Grace stared out the window, where people passed on their way to work.

"But he didn't and that's that. I can remember when I was a boy and got my first bike. No way was I going to run home to mother because I'd fallen off it. I was having too much fun. And he's had fun, too."

"You weren't a hemophiliac."

"No, but he is a boy. This isn't getting us anywhere—what'll we do? There has to be some doctor we can ask to help."

"Someone we can trust," Grace said.

"Not just someone we can trust. Someone who'll bend the rules. And that takes care of Doctor Anderson. He's a good

8

doctor, but he sure does go by the book. No exceptions." He pounded the table.

Grace turned from the window and began to cry. "It seems so hopeless. And so wrong, with all the doctors and medical facilities we have here in the United States, that there's no one to care for a little boy with hemophilia."

"It is wrong," Jon agreed. "But there's nothing we can do about it. Or at least, I can't think of anything."

"Maybe an idea will come to us today."

"Maybe. But I'll have to leave now." He kissed her and held her for a moment. "Stephen's sleeping a bit later this morning. Maybe his hip doesn't bother him as much."

"Don't forget," Grace said, "you're to call me if anything turns up, anything at all. Please be careful about what you say on the phone."

Jonathan and Grace Stanton had been married eight years, the first marriage for each of them. Jonathan was employed in the corporate offices of Stern International. Grace didn't work outside their home.

"I'd rather have you bring up our child than turn it over to the day-care center," Jon had said when he learned his wife was pregnant.

"Not it—shim," Grace said with a laugh. "The baby will be human, not a thing. Just because we have a woman President doesn't mean I have to work while someone else takes care of my child. Maybe I'll want to work outside the home some day, or have to. If I do, I will, but not the first few years."

Stephen was born at home, at Grace's insistence. An old woman in their church, who had been a midwife in the West Virginia mountains years before, delivered him.

"Such a perfect little fellow," the midwife said as she handed him to Grace. "Look at his fingers and toes."

But he wasn't perfect. He bruised easily and without obvious cause. Grace noticed it when he was several months old and mentioned it to Jon.

"See here—on his arm. I've watched him very carefully, and I can't explain the bruises he gets. Jon, I'm afraid he has

9

hemophilia. You know that it runs in my father's family, and a daughter can pass it on. Oh, Jon, I'm so sorry."

"Were you afraid this would happen?" Jon asked. "Is that why you insisted on having the baby at home?"

Grace was silent.

"Well, thank God that we have him. I hate to think, if you'd done it the regular way, gone into the hospital— We'll just have to treat him with special care, gently. And when he gets older— but why think of that?"

Now he was older and they were forced to think of it.

STERN INTERNATIONAL was one of the first companies to be licensed by the Department of Energy to manufacture the radically new self-contained energy units for single-family dwellings. These narrow cylindrical generators, powered by a low-level atomic reactor and weighing a ton, were lowered into wells two hundred feet below ground level, much like submersible water pumps. With a life expectancy of thirty years, a unit supplied enough electrical energy by direct conversion for one house's heating, cooling and other energy needs.

Jon Stanton was employed by Stern's marketing department, in sales research. He liked his work, for which he had been trained at the University of Pennsylvania's Wharton School, and ordinarily found no difficulty concentrating on his current projects.

Today was different. Today he was distracted, edgy with the word processor who brought him a completed report, unable to focus his thoughts on the weekly sales analysis. Several times he picked up the phone, held it a moment, then put it down again.

Nothing would be gained by calling home. The problem was there, it wouldn't change—it would only get worse. He no longer went over the possibilities in his mind; it was useless, and only resulted in a crescendo of fear.

Doctor Allen. He finally admitted the one hope, the one possibility of avoiding total disaster. He had known they would ultimately turn in this direction, but had submerged the thought. Now it surfaced.

He spoke the name into the phone, "Philip J. Allen, M.D.," and immediately was connected. He saw the familiar face on the videophone screen.

"Philip Allen here."

"Doctor Allen, this is Jon Stanton."

"Hello, Jon. Are you calling me about the church? Can I call you back?"

"No, it's sort of personal."

"You're calling me professionally?"

"Yes, I am."

"But you're not on my patient list, are you?"

"No, but—"

"Sorry. There's nothing I can do for you. Please take up any professional matter with your own designated physician."

"But, Doctor Allen, this is something different, an unusual situation. I'm calling you because we're in the same church. Surely you're willing to listen to a brother Christian."

There was a long pause.

"I am willing to listen to you, but I can't help you. No matter what the problem is—if it's professional help you're asking for. You know how they are about such matters."

"Will you at least listen to our—my problem?"

"Yes, I will. But meet me in the park across from the medical center, not at my office. Four o'clock this afternoon."

"I'll be there. And thank you, sir."

Now he phoned home. Stephen answered.

11

"Hello, Stephen, How's my boy today?"

"Hi, daddy. My leg doesn't hurt like it did yesterday. When can I start riding my bike again?"

"Hey, that's good news, son. But no bike riding for a few days, anyway. Now may I speak to mother?—Hello, Grace. I wanted you to know that it looks as if the deal is going through. I'll be discussing it with my brother Allen this afternoon." He was guarded in what he said.

"That's wonderful, honey. I'll be praying. I'm sure he'll be able to advise you."

"He has to. Otherwise—" His voice trailed off. Both were silent for a long moment.

"Good-bye, Jon."

He left the office early, walking rather than riding to the park. He wanted time to think, to compose himself for what could be a difficult confrontation. It all depended on Philip Allen. Doctor Philip Allen.

Strange, he thought, how you could be with people week after week, break bread at the Lord's table with them, exchange words after the service, and yet not know them. You'd think the pressure for survival, the fact that they were a little flock would pull people together—make them mean something to each other. But somehow it didn't, except in rare instances.

He knew there were some people who seemed to live in the upper room, like first-century Christians—sharing everything, not holding back. They became vulnerable to each other and thus less vulnerable to the enemy. You told them everything and they cried with you, prayed with you, lived your despair. And somehow they gave you a transfusion of hope.

But hope wasn't enough now. Another kind of transfusion was needed. Would Doctor Allen agree to give it? He had to.

Philip Allen . . . how little he knew about him. Only that he was a doctor, that he was married—for the second time—that he had one son in his late teens who no longer came to church.

Strange that he knew nothing about Philip Allen profession-ally. It was as if he checked his professional life at the door to the church.

The thought troubled him. For the first time he fully opened his mind to the possibility that Doctor Allen would be unwilling to act. Where would they turn?

He stopped walking, his heart pounded, he suddenly was very warm.

"Dear God, make him act. Make him see our desperate need and be moved by it—moved with compassion. Keep him from being a—" He paused at the word "coward," then changed it. "Keep him from being afraid of what might happen. I don't really blame him if he's afraid. But help him to be touched by Stephen's need and to act."

Just before four, he arrived at the park, entering it by the gate near the medical center. He sat down on a bench and waited.

"Hello. I hope you've not been waiting long." It was Philip Allen.

"Thanks for giving me your time, Doctor Allen. I'll try to be brief."

"Let's move out into the open, away from this bench and these trees. Have you combed your suit recently?"

"Just before I left the office. There was nothing."

"Those new microdot transmitters are difficult to find. One of my patients stuck one on my lapel the other day. She leaned against me just for a moment, as if she were faint. After she left, I discovered it. Then I had to decide whether it was more risky to leave it there and guard everything I said, everywhere I went during the next few days, or flush it down the toilet."

"What did you do?"

Obviously pleased with himself, the doctor answered, "I put it on the lab coat of my most politicized colleague. They'll hear nothing but what they like to hear from him and his contacts. And the beautiful thing is that they'll blame my patient for the mistake. —Let's stop here and talk. You want to tell me about your son."

"How did you know? Did someone tell you? Only a few people know about him."

"I've watched him since he was born. I first noticed a bruise on his hand when he was several months old. Knowing how

13

careful your wife is, the next time I saw bruising I drew a tentative conclusion. Then there was one Sunday he had his arm in a sling. That sling seemed to be around for an awful long time. And last Sunday I noticed he wasn't in church and neither was your wife."

"It's been that obvious? Anyway, that makes it easier."

"Not necessarily. I have a question: How did they miss it in the prenatal examination? And especially when he was born? Things like that just don't happen here—maybe down in Mississippi, but not here."

"Grace had the baby at home. One of the old ladies in the church came in and helped with the delivery."

"Damn. Excuse me. I guess that isn't a Christian response."

"The word doesn't bother me. I hope you're referring to the system, though."

"The system, as you call it, is responsible for near-zero level of infant deaths. And childhood, teenage, adult ones, too. Perhaps even more important, the quality of life. No Down's syndrome, no deformed people, no diabetic children, no cystic fibrosis. This is an improvement of historic importance. When I went to medical school—only twenty-five years ago—we still learned about those conditions and treated them. Yes, and hemophilia. Now, thank God, they've been wiped out; they're just as much off the books as polio was then. So we doctors can spend our time maintaining the health of whole persons, not treating handicapped people and the chronically ill."

"Then you do know how to treat hemophilia. Stephen's a hemophiliac, and he desperately needs help. You can give it to him. We have nowhere else to turn."

"He is ill because of an illegal act on your part. You and your wife were under obligation to observe the law, a law which says that the fetus must be analyzed *in utero* and aborted if defective. You not only disregarded that law, you also failed to have the newborn examined for defect. Had you done either of those things, you would not be faced with this problem today."

"But we didn't, and we do have the problem. And it's critical."

"Where's he bleeding?"

"Into the hip. It's swollen and very painful."

"What do you want me to do?"

"Whatever will bring him through this without crippling. And without the authorities finding out about his condition."

"What kind of hemophilia is it? Classic or Christmas?"

"Christmas, according to Grace's father. He says his brother died as the result of a bleeding incident when he was in his twenties."

"When I was in medical school, they still treated hemophilia. They had cases to treat. But today there are no cases, so there's no treatment. They no longer isolate the blood factor that enables coagulation to take place. I couldn't find it anywhere in the United States. I'd have to go, maybe, to Russia for it. They're not yet up to us medically. They still have cases."

"Isn't there anything else that helps? Blood transfusions, plasma?"

"Plasma would probably do it, if I recall my hematology correctly. But we don't treat hemophilia today. That's a thing of the past."

"What you mean is that for you to do anything would be illegal, and might get you into trouble with the authorities." He said it without bitterness.

"No, I didn't mean to say that, although it does happen to be true. I could be removed from medical practice if they found out. My certification would be taken away. I might even be sent to a detention camp. This is an illegal act you are asking me to perform. Do you understand that?"

"Of course I do. God knows I do. But it is at the same time a Christian act."

"Can anything that's contrary to the law be Christian? Hasn't God placed our rulers over us, as Paul tells us in Romans? Are you advocating antinomianism?"

For a moment, Jon didn't trust himself to say anything. He

15

remembered Stephen's voice on the phone, "Daddy, my leg doesn't hurt so much today." Then he spoke.

"What does the law say now, today? What are Grace and I to do with the problem that's staring us in the face?"

"Get your doctor to admit him to the hospital. They will then make a complete diagnosis of his case."

"And if it is really hemophilia—as you and I know it is—what then?"

"You can cross that bridge when you come to it, if you come to it."

"But I want to know what's on the other side of the bridge before I bring him up to it. What could happen?"

"We have clearly defined procedures. I would prefer going over them with you when you are not so emotionally upset. Actually, I'd prefer to have your own physician go over them with you. But since you want an answer right now, I'll try to explain."

The doctor paused, looked at his watch, then continued. "As you know, the health of a society is of prime importance. We haven't gotten where we are without a lot of hard work and disciplined thinking and—for some—sacrifice. All of those concepts are compatible with your Christian convictions, I feel sure.

"We could regress with deceptive ease, considering the hard road by which we have progressed to this point. A bit of softness, a permissive attitude, and twenty years of improved health, dramatically improved health, could go down the tube. Only let a few handicapped people live, let them procreate, ease up on the fetal examinations and abortions—you can see where we'd be. So when we discover a congenital condition such as hemophilia, we cannot overlook it. We must act. There are procedures we must follow.

"I really must be getting home. Perhaps we can continue this some other time, although I don't think there is anything I can add to what I've already said."

"You mean that if Stephen really has hemophilia—as we know he does, you and I—he'll be sent to the organ factory. He'll be killed by you doctors. That's what you mean, isn't it?"

16

"I know the strain this situation imposes on you," Doctor Allen replied. "I have nothing to do with the Center for Life Support Systems—the organ factory, as people call it. There are specialists who attend the patients there."

"Patients? Corpses. Brainless corpses. Why don't you come right out and tell me they'll take Stephen to the thanotel, that his higher brain center will be killed but his lower brain will be kept alive? That he'll be taken from there to the organ factory and placed on a slab next to a thousand other brainless babies and children." His voice grew louder; the doctor looked around to see if anyone was listening.

"Why don't you tell me that Stephen, my son Stephen, would spend the next few years there, being fed intravenously, being kept alive, while they removed one organ after another for transplant. A kidney—not both, or he'd die a second time, really die this time. An arm, a leg, teeth, arteries, a hand, an ear, two eyes, a gall bladder, one lung, skin for grafting—skin from most of his body, hair for some politician or TV star. Then finally—all at the same time—the other lung, the other kidney, his heart, in one great *coup de grace*.

"Why don't you have the guts to tell me what would happen to Stephen if we took him to the hospital like you say we should? You gutless mach."

He turned his back on the doctor and walked, almost ran, out of the park.

During the few blocks to the subway, and during the ride home his actions were unthinking, automatic; when he walked in the door, it was as if he had come that very moment from his encounter with Philip Allen in the park.

"Daddy!" Stephen called to him from the big chair. "Come here. Look at what I've been reading."

He went over and lifted the boy very carefully, then sat down with him on his lap. He didn't trust himself to speak.

"You're holding me too tight, daddy. Are you crying? Mother, daddy's crying."

He felt the boy's warmth through his clothing, buried his face in his hair, gently rubbed his hip.

17

"We waited supper for you." Grace leaned over to kiss her husband. In that moment she could read what was in his face, fresh despair, beyond anything she had seen there before. The hope that he had shown on the videophone was gone, she realized with grief and foreboding. "Maybe you'll want to wash first," she suggested quietly. "I'll put the food on the table while you're getting ready."

"I don't feel like eating."

"Of course you don't, but you should. Go get washed—maybe lift Stephen over to the table first. Here, I'll put a pillow on the chair."

He stood up with the boy in his arms, then put him gently down on the chair. He kissed the soft hair on top of his head and went upstairs to the bathroom.

"Don't be too long," she called, "or it'll get cold."

In the bathroom he was alone, totally alone for the first time since he had left Philip Allen. He began to cry; great sobs shook his body. He flushed the toilet to cover the sound. He looked at the hands that had just held his son, stroked his hair, touched his hip; then he broke down still more. He flushed the toilet again. He realized that he was unable to stop crying.

"Dear, are you all right?" He heard Grace's voice outside the door. "I'm coming in."

"Don't," he said. "I'll be out in a minute."

She opened the door, looked at him, and ran the few steps to his side. She gathered him into her arms, kissed him, put her cheek next to his cheek. He felt her soft breasts, smelled the freshness of her hair.

"My dearest Jon," she said. "Oh, how I love you. And so does Stephen."

"Do you know what I called Philip Allen? Doctor Philip Allen?" He pressed his fingers into his eyes.

"What?"

"A gutless mach."

"If you called him that, I guess that's what he is. Now here's a washcloth—let's get some cold water on it and wash your face. There, you should feel better."

18

"I do. Not the cold water, but you. You're always here when I need you. You know, he had already guessed that Stephen was a hemophiliac. From when his arm was in a sling."

She took his hand and led him to the table where Stephen was patiently waiting. Patience was one of Stephen's virtues; he never complained.

"Stephen, will you pray tonight?"

"Sure, dad. Dear Jesus, thank you for this food. Help my leg not to hurt. Amen.

"Daddy, I'm glad you're not crying any more."

That evening, after Stephen was in bed, Jon told Grace about the conversation with Philip Allen, only omitting any reference to what would happen at the thanotel and the organ factory.

"Say we did take Stevie to the hospital," she asked, "what would they be able to do for him?"

"Nothing. That's precisely the point. They'd confirm the diagnosis of hemophilia—which you and I know already—and let it go at that. We'd be no further ahead than we are now."

Grace frowned, "Can't Doctor Allen do anything for Stephen? It seems to me that with him being in the church, and so ready to talk about Christian things, he ought to feel some responsibility for our little boy."

"I thought so too. But he doesn't. He just talks about how we've behaved illegally all along, and implies that Stephen should have been aborted as a fetus or sent to the organ factory after he was born."

She shuddered. "And he's supposed to be a Christian."

"He probably is. I guess I can't blame him for refusing to do something that might endanger his career, maybe even threaten his freedom. That's asking pretty much of any man."

"But not of a Christian," Grace replied. "Jesus said that we should be happy when we're persecuted for doing what's right— that we're in good company when that happens."

"What if he thinks obeying the government is right, and letting Stephen live would be wrong?"

"If he thinks that, he's sick, morally sick," Grace said. "He

19

doesn't belong at the Lord's table—he ought to be excluded, along with unbelievers."

"I only wish we'd never had to find out what kind of a doctor—or Christian—Philip Allen is. Did I hear something?" He moved to the stairway. "I thought I heard— Yes, Stephen's crying." He bounded up the stairs, followed closely by Grace.

"Mother, it hurts. My leg hurts. Don't lift me, daddy—" as Jon put his arms under him. "You'll make it hurt more."

"Dear, I'll put some ice in the ice pack, and we'll put that next to your leg. Then it'll feel better." She went down to the kitchen.

The little boy continued to cry, softly. Looking at him lying there, so small, so helpless, so vulnerable, Jon felt his bitterness toward Philip Allen turning suddenly to hatred. Or was it hatred toward God? Who was really responsible for Stephen's condition? Philip Allen might be able to help the little boy if he was willing to take the risk and do the right thing; God could have prevented it in the first place, could stop the pain that made his little boy cry, could stop it right now—this very instant—could totally heal, if he wanted to. Why wasn't God moved by the child's tears as he was, as Grace was? The Bible said that God pities those who fear him, like a father pities his children. But how could this be true if he didn't pity a little six-year-old boy whose hip was hurting so much, whose whole future was at stake?

"Here's the ice pack, Stevie," Grace said. "Let me lift you just a bit, and put it next to your leg. There now, it will soon feel better." She leaned over and kissed him on the cheek. "I'll stay here until you go to sleep." Jon brought her a chair.

"Jon," she said, "why don't you pray for Stephen and then go to bed."

He prayed, but his heart wasn't in it. Afterward, as he undressed, he hoped that Grace hadn't noticed. But she probably had. He had a hard time getting to sleep.

Grace sat in a rocking chair beside Stephen's bed, softly singing, "All through the night, all through the night, my Savior will be watching over me . . ." The old chair made a

20

creaking sound as she rocked back and forth. It had belonged to her grandmother. She held Stephen's hand.

"Mother, hold me on your lap. It won't hurt as much if you hold me."

She picked the warm little boy up in her arms, molding the ice pack around his hip on her lap. She covered him with a blanket from the bed. Stephen asked her to tell him a story; she did, stretching it out. Back and forth, back and forth she rocked. She wasn't sleepy, but she prayed that her little boy would soon go to sleep. Sleep helped anything heal, she knew that.

She remembered holding him when he was a baby. What a happy baby he had been, seldom crying unless there was a cause. Jon and she had received such joy from watching him grow, helping him grow and mature. His first step—how happy she'd been that both Jon and she were there for it. And yet, with all her happiness during those first years, there was that lurking dread of what might happen if the bleeding problem was discovered. Could she handle it? Could Jon? Would it bring them even closer together, or was it possible that they might be pulled apart by the crisis—if it wasn't resolved? But it would be, she was sure of that.

When Stephen finally slept, she continued to hold him and rock in the chair. But finally she laid him in the bed with great care, turned off the light in the room, and went to bed.

The next morning when Jon awoke, the sun was up, birds were singing, a breeze made the curtains dance. *What a beautiful day,* he thought. He turned and felt Grace, still asleep. He was filled with a sense of peace.

Then it hit him, like a bomb exploding in his brain, destroying his peace, his joy of life and living.

Stephen.

His son. The hip injury.

Jon got out of bed quickly and went into Stephen's room. The ice pack was on the floor, covers were at the foot of the bed—and the little boy was sleeping peacefully.

"Thank you, God," he prayed silently. "And forgive me for

21

my feelings toward you and toward Philip Allen last night. I don't think it's just that my little boy is feeling no pain this morning—maybe it is, but if it is, and my bitterness—even worse feelings—come back later, I pray right now for you to forgive me them. I want to believe, I really want to believe that you are hurt as much as I am, as Grace is, by Stephen's pain. I want to believe that you aren't just a giant computer running the universe, but that you cry even, that you pity Stephen—and Grace and me—even if you can't, or won't do anything about it. Like in the bathroom last night, I want a Father I can lean on. I don't want a great big computer in the sky. There are enough computers here on earth. And men who act like computers. Like Philip Allen."

Stephen turned over. His eyes opened for a moment, he murmured, "Hi, daddy," and went back to sleep.

Jon went into the bathroom where he showered and shaved. Back in the bedroom, while he dressed, he listened to the bird songs, went over to the window and looked out at the small bed of chrysanthemums, radiant in the sun's bright light.

This was an important day at Stern International, he remembered. Today they would discuss marketing plans for the next year; his own research would be the basis of decisions which would commit hundreds of thousands of dollars to advertising. He wondered if he'd be able to keep his mind on marketing matters, knowing that they were heading toward disaster at home.

"Have you seen Stevie?" Grace spoke from the bed, her voice deep with sleep.

"Yes, I just looked in on him. He must be feeling better. At least he's sleeping, and doesn't seem to have any pain. It's a beautiful day. Go back to sleep—I'll get my own breakfast. You must have been up pretty late."

"I was. He stopped crying just a little while after we put the ice pack on. But he couldn't seem to get to sleep. So I told him a story, a long one. Thanks for letting me sleep." She turned the pillow over, punched it a few times, and closed her eyes.

22

Jon went down to the kitchen, where he had coffee and orange juice. As he was leaving the house, he turned back to the kitchen. Making each letter clearly, so that Stephen could read it, he printed, "God loves us" on the old-fashioned chalkboard that hung on the wall beside the sink. Underneath, he wrote in his hard-to-read script, "I hope." Grace could read that.

The next few days passed with little change in Stephen's condition. His hip did not pain him as it had the week before, or at least he didn't cry as frequently. But it was getting stiff.

Now it was Sunday, a rainy, windy Sunday.

"You go to church this morning," Jon said. "I'll stay home with Stephen."

After a moment's hesitation, Grace agreed. "All right. But I wish you'd go instead."

"Do you think I need it more than you do? To be truthful, I'm afraid of what I might say to Philip Allen, Doctor Philip Allen."

"Be careful," she said with quiet emphasis. "You're a Christian, and you know how easy it is to forget to love the brothers."

"If he is a brother. At this point I'm not sure."

"All the more reason you should be careful of how you feel toward him. It's not just other Christians we're to love—Jesus said we should love our enemies."

He laughed bitterly. "I'll be careful. It's just that if I were in the service this morning, and Doctor Philip Allen was there, I'm afraid of what I'd do."

"You wouldn't do anything. Now remember to put fresh ice in the ice pack about an hour from now."

She stepped briskly through the door and walked down the street, an umbrella protecting her from the heavy rain. She was chilled by the time she reached the church building, a structure that was a half-century old, with stained glass windows seldom used in church structures any more. The service had already begun. She waited until a hymn was announced, then hurriedly sat down in a pew at the back.

The church was independent, without any denominational relationship. "Independent of everybody and everything except God," Pastor Snyder frequently said.

Only recently, this pride in independence had begun to bother Jon. "Maybe it would be good if we were a bit more dependent," he said to Grace, "dependent on each other, and dependent on Christians in other churches. I think he really means independent of everybody and everything except Jerry Snyder."

Grace was reminded of her husband's comment as she listened to the pastor announce the morning Scripture reading. She had disagreed with Jon, had said that he was too critical. But now his words came back to her.

"All you people have your Bibles, turn to Exodus twenty-five, verse one. This Sunday we are embarking on a study of the tabernacle. Exodus twenty-five, verse one." Mechanically Grace opened her Bible, noting as she often did the gentle sound of pages being turned throughout the sanctuary. She found her place as the pastor began to read, "'And the Lord spake unto Moses, saying . . .'" Suddenly she closed her Bible.

Here they were, at the biggest crisis of their lives, and they were alone. Maybe Jon was right, the church needed more dependence—certainly she and Jon did. But she had to be careful that a root of bitterness didn't spring up in her. Jon did, too.

"'And thou shalt put the staves into the rings by the sides of the ark, that the ark may be borne with them. The staves shall be in the rings of the ark . . . And thou shalt make two cherubim of gold . . .'"

Staves and rings and cherubim. She looked about her distractedly. Everyone else's attention seemed to be given to the reading. Staves and rings and cherubim.

In this calm place, removed from her storm, she tried to shut off the part of her mind that was obsessed with Stephen her son, the son of her womb; to no avail. Not part, she realized, but her whole mind was taken up with it.

Then the reading was over, and the pastor announced a hymn. The organ began to play.

24

The organ. She looked at the pipes that rose above and behind the pulpit chairs. She concentrated on the darkness behind the pipes.

The organ factory. Stephen. And the pastor was talking about staves and rings and cherubim. Staves and rings and cherubim, when the government was going to take her little boy away from her . . . and kill him. No, they wouldn't. God wouldn't let them. Stephen would get well. She was sure of it.

Pastor Snyder announced a closing hymn. The words made her suddenly alert, a conscious part of the worshiping group: "My Savior returns to heal every hurt, to meet every need, to right every wrong." Wouldn't it be wonderful, she thought, if Jesus came back today, or tonight? No more need for a doctor or ice packs or pressure bandages. No more need to be afraid of what the government would do to Stephen.

Then it was over. She spoke a few words to the people on either side of her. She lowered her head and went out the side door, out into the cold rain, avoiding the pastor who was standing at the back.

After dinner, when she had put Stephen to bed for a nap, Grace said, "I feel like a nap, too."

"Go ahead," Jon said. "I'll get back to my reading. Or call up a game on the videocomputer."

"No, Jon. I want you to come to bed with me. I don't want to be alone. If you won't, I'll stay up with you and watch the game."

"All right," Jon agreed. "I could stand some extra sleep."

But they didn't sleep.

"Jon, I think Stephen's hip will get all right without anything being done to it. Don't you feel that way, too?"

"Were Philip Allen and his wife in church today?"

"No, at least I didn't see them. If they had been, I don't know what I'd have done. Or said. But don't you think Stephen will get all right?"

"No, I don't," Jon said firmly. "Not without attention to that hip. I wish I could, but— What was the sermon about?"

"The tabernacle."

25

"The tabernacle?"

"Yes, staves and rings and cherubim. Stop that. We came up here to sleep."

"But we're talking."

"I know. But somehow it doesn't seem right to enjoy ourselves when Stephen—"

The doorbell rang.

"Saved by the bell," Jon said as he jumped out of bed and put on his clothes. "I wonder who that could be."

"Well, you'd better hurry or they won't wait."

"Why don't you get up and go to the door?" Jon said as he pulled the sheet off her.

"You scoundrel." She pulled the sheet back up.

A few moments later he returned. "Get dressed, we've got company. The Swansons—Norm and Ruth."

"I'll be right down. I wonder what brought them out on an ugly afternoon like this." Grace dressed hurriedly as Jon went back downstairs.

"We're sorry we interrupted your nap," Ruth said when Grace came down the stairs.

"Don't worry about that," Grace reassured her. "We were talking; I don't think we'd have slept anyway."

"We were sort of worried that something was wrong here," Norm explained. They were a few years older than Jon and Grace. "We noticed that you were alone at church this morning, Grace. We thought something might be wrong, someone sick or something like that, you know. So we decided to come over for a little visit, since we didn't get a chance to talk to you after the service and find out."

"I ran off right away," Grace said. "I was in a hurry to get home. Stephen's been down with a bad hip."

"I'm sorry," Ruth said. "How is he now? Is his hip any better?"

Having admitted the fact of Stephen's injury, Grace, with a nod of reassurance from Jon, decided to explain its seriousness. She was sure that Norm and Ruth could be trusted with their secret.

"So you see, we have a really big problem on our hands," she concluded.

"Why, that's not a big problem," Ruth stated flatly. "Not for God. There's nothing—absolutely nothing—too hard for him. All you need to do is have faith."

"Have faith for what?" Jon asked, although he suspected what the answer would be.

"Why, that God will heal Stephen. Jesus said that our faith can remove mountains, so surely it's able to heal a little boy's hip."

The silence that followed was becoming embarrassing, when Grace said, "I have faith in God, but I'm not sure it's big enough for either a mountain or a hip. And at this moment, Stephen's hemophilia seems even bigger than a mountain."

"Well, I'll tell you one thing," Norm said, "you won't find the faith at the church we're all in. Not by a long shot."

"Where will you find it?" Jon was curious, for while he had been somewhat critical of their church just to Grace—for its self-sufficiency and lack of fellowship—he had never faulted it for any lack of faith.

"In the small house church we're a part of. That's our secret, like yours about Stephen's being a bleeder—something that Jerry Snyder and the other members of the church don't know about. Nor the government—it's unregistered. It meets every Sunday night. The people come from several different churches, and they're all down to business with the Lord. It's really a choice fellowship."

"Where do you meet?" Jon asked.

"You just say the word; any Sunday night we'll come and pick you up. Take you there. And if you want to have us anoint Stephen for healing—"

"Thanks, Norm, we'll remember that offer."

"Norman, we'd better be getting home."

"Yes, dear. Now don't forget my offer. I really mean it."

After they left, Grace sighed.

"Tiring, wasn't it?" Jon said.

27

"Yes, but they were the only ones concerned enough to come over to see us. Don't forget that."

"I won't. It's just that—" He stopped without finishing what he was going to say. In fact, he didn't know what he was going to say. The only thing he knew was that he had a vague, uneasy feeling.

"Let's get the candles out for supper," Grace suggested. "And neither of us go to church—although you can if you want to. You haven't been today."

"I didn't plan to go. I want a quiet supper in front of the fireplace. I'll build a fire. Then I want to hold Stephen in my lap while I read to him."

"We'll take turns," Grace said with a wan smile.

AT ONE o'clock on Monday afternoon, just after Jon had returned to the office from lunch, his phone rang.

"Jon Stanton speaking," he answered as he pressed the receive switch for a videoscreen image.

"Does the name Allen mean anything to you?"

The man evidently didn't want to reveal his identity, since he was holding down the display button at his end of the line. Jon immediately did the same, though not before his image had been received by his caller.

"I don't think it does," he replied, speaking quite deliberately.

"Are you sure? Does the name mean anything to you if I say 'injury'?"

"Maybe so, why?" Whatever risk there was to Stephen or

Doctor Allen or himself, Jon had to respond to the question.

"All right. Can you meet me in the park across from the medical center in about an hour? I'll be sitting on the third bench on the left side as you enter the park. Just stand in front of the bench, facing away from it. Then I'll get up and walk to an open area farther into the park. You follow, and when I stop, tell me the type it is. Did you get that?"

"What type it is?"

"Yes. See you in an hour."

Jon called Grace and told her about the unexpected appointment. "I just had a phone call. I don't know who it was, but Allen told him about the deal and he wants to talk to me about it. Please don't worry if I get home a little late. 'By, love you." After taking off his suit coat and combing it with his fingers, then brushing his pants to make sure he was clean of microdot transmitters, he left his office. Instead of taking the subway, Jon decided he would walk the seven blocks to the medical center to keep from being scanned by the subway platform cameras. He felt sneaky dodging those cameras, but at least the Department of Transportation wouldn't have a record of his trip to the medical center if something went wrong.

He wondered who could have called him. He had to be wary, or he might get Philip Allen in trouble for listening to his problem. Not that he cared much for that chicken-hearted doctor anyway, but Allen might inform on Stephen, or himself—as he obviously already had. And yet the voice hadn't sounded like that of a troublemaker, a government agent. It had sounded warm, perhaps even compassionate. Or was that wishful thinking? At any rate, he must be careful of what he said.

He waited outside the medical center until almost two, then crossed to the park. Two men were sitting on the third bench on the left; one, who looked Jewish, was wearing a rumpled brown suit, had his legs crossed and was intently reading a newspaper. The other man had on a sport shirt, open at the neck, and was glaring at his tennis shoes.

Jon paused in front of the bench, turned his back to the two men and looked at his watch.

29

After a few moments, the man in the suit got up, stuffed the paper under his arm, and walked at quite a rapid pace farther into the park. He left the sidewalk and went across the grass, stopping at a spot where there were no trees or benches or people nearby.

Jon followed him at a discreet distance. When the man stopped, he walked alongside him and spoke softly: "Christmas type."

"Good," the man replied.

He had been right about the voice, but that must not lead him to be careless.

"Did you comb your suit?"

"Before I left the office."

"So did I. But I think I'd better examine the side that was next to my companion on the bench. Please stand close to me so no one can see." He ran his hand along the left arm and side of his suit, and down his trousers. Jon noticed how long and slender his fingers were.

"I guess I'm clean. Silly game, but a lot is at stake. Something very precious is at stake: the life of a child."

A warning bell rang in Jon's mind. "I really don't know what you're talking about," he said.

"Yes, you do. Come on, it's safe—I'm safe—don't worry. I won't report you; maybe I can help you."

"How?" Uncertainty replaced the suspicion in Jon's voice. But he would not permit the tone to indicate hope.

"I'm a medical colleague of Philip Allen. Several of us were having coffee this morning, and he told us about your situation. Actually, I think he was looking for somebody to tell him that he had done the right thing. Maybe it was for protection that he told it, in case anything came up in the future. We gave him the confirmation he wanted, but later—just before lunch—I casually asked him for the name of the man who had requested his help. Don't worry, I didn't alert him to anything. I told him I wondered if it could be one of the families on my list about whom I've had suspicions. He told me your name, and I took a chance calling you. Fortunately, he told me you worked in the city, so I located your business number in central computer. Your job must be fairly important for your company to list you. I'm glad it is; otherwise I'd have been at a dead end. I'd like to help, if you'll trust me. But to do that I'll have to know exactly what the condition is—both background and present problem."

"How do I know I can trust you not to blurt out my name like Philip Allen did?"

"You don't. There's no way you can know, except possibly by looking into my eyes. But if you really can't trust me, you've already lost the game anyway. I can get your home phone number—I know it's unlisted, like all the rest; but if I'm an agent of the government, I can easily manage it. And from there it's all downhill to the organ factory for your son. By the way, what's his name? How old is he?"

"Stephen. He's six years old," Jon replied.

"I should tell you who I am, to alleviate your fears. I am Price Berkowitz, I'm Jewish, and a general surgeon, and I can at least to some extent match your risk. I too have a son who is in constant danger of being sent to the Center for Life Support Systems. Don't think they treat us doctors and our families different from anyone else. They don't. My child has a condition known as Tay-Sachs disease. It causes severe brain damage, blindness—my little fellow is already affected this way—and usually, by age three or four, death. Some of us Jews whose ancestors came from eastern Europe carry it in our genes as your wife carries Christmas-type hemophilia in hers. Only it takes two carriers, both the man and the woman, to bring about Tay-Sachs. Fortunately—some would say unfortunately—it wasn't discovered during the fetal examination, or even after birth. So I myself diagnosed it for the first time about a year ago. —By the way, how'd they miss the hemophilia condition in your wife's fetal examination, and the baby's examination after birth?"

"She never reported her pregnancy and Stephen was born at home."

"That's a new wrinkle. I didn't know anybody was born at home anymore. I salute you for your courage. And your wife. But how did you get him registered?"

31

Jon paused only for a moment. He was in so deep already that it didn't seem to matter if he revealed everything. "In our church, there's a woman who works in the bureau of vital statistics. She took care of registration for us, and getting Stephen a Social Security number."

"May God reward her as He did the midwives who saved Moses from the Egyptian killer government. Now that we've exchanged enough information that we're forced to trust each other, tell me about Stephen's recent incident."

"About a week ago he fell while he was playing. Riding his bike. Later that night he complained of pain in his hip. We applied pressure and cold at once, but it was too late by then—"

"Or more likely, damage to the tissue was too extensive to make any difference, even if you'd applied ice at once."

"Whatever it was, the situation hasn't improved, and we're afraid that his leg will get stiff at the hip and he'll be permanently crippled."

"Bleeding into the joint of course can have that result. And if he's crippled—"

"He'll be sent to the hospital," Jon finished the sentence.

"And if he's admitted to the hospital, he'll be sent to the Center—the organ factory—after they diagnose the condition as Christmas disease. So you're in between the devil and the deep blue sea."

"Exactly. . . . Can you help us?"

Doctor Berkowitz didn't seem to hear.

"Isn't this a magnificent society we're a part of? No cripples, no blind people, no institutions for the retarded, no homes for old people, just the Center for Life Support Systems. No weak people—only strong. Survival of the fit, the beautiful people. And taxes have been lowered, because we no longer have to support the helpless. They even support us by providing blood for transfusions, tissues and organs for transplant. For the first time in history we have a society of the strong, right here in America. Hitler aimed at it years ago, but he missed. Now we've aimed too, and we've hit the bull's-eye. God, how I hate it. How I hate doing transplant operations. Every kidney I implant, I see

32

my son, my dear defective son, brain-dead at the Center for Life Support Systems. . . . You know, don't you, that children grow up at the Center? They don't stay infants or six years old. Those living corpses are fed nutrients, hormones and chemicals so that they achieve physical maturity. So your son or mine could still be providing limbs and organs ten years from now. Do they feel pain? Who knows . . . or cares? What we do know is that no anesthesia is used in removing organs. Anesthesia is too likely to interfere with the brain's autonomic system—and cause real, final death."

Jon lowered his head.

"Excuse me for letting loose. If you didn't know those things, forget them. That's a stupid statement because you never will, never can. But at least you know now what the stakes are in this tremendous gamble you and I are taking for our sons."

"Can you do anything for Stephen?"

"Yes, I can. That is, I'm pretty sure I can. Tell me your address; I'll come to your home tonight around nine o'clock."

"We live in Wayne, 517 Auden Avenue."

"Good. That's only fifteen or twenty minutes from where I live. See you at nine." He walked rapidly away toward the medical center.

Jon hesitated a moment, then decided to go home instead of returning to the office. He wouldn't be late getting home, but Grace would be anxious to know, and he couldn't wait to share the unexpected, hopeful new development as soon as possible. And anyway, he'd just about get back to the office when he'd have to leave again.

So a child could grow old at the organ factory. A child's body could mature, awaiting the removal of parts. He shuddered. He had never seen the institution; even if he'd wanted to, they'd never allow anyone but experienced medical personnel inside. But he imagined the rows of silent, unmoving bodies, looking without seeing—if they still had eyes. He imagined Stephen in his late teens, grown tall. . . .

Enough. He had to discipline his mind. Those thoughts running wild could not help anything—they could only keep him from the sort of cool, dispassionate thinking that was urgently needed.

On arriving home, he told Grace everything he knew about Doctor Berkowitz, and everything the doctor had said, omitting only the fresh light—or darkness—he had thrown on the organ factory.

"Do you really think you can trust this doctor?" Grace asked.

"Yes, I think we can. You can draw your own conclusions tonight, but the whole thing came out of the blue so completely that I think God must be in it. And there's no one else to turn to."

Shortly before nine o'clock, the bell rang. Jon saw that it was Price Berkowitz when he looked in the security scanner. He opened the door and noticed that the doctor was carrying a shopping bag. He wore the same rumpled brown suit he'd been wearing that afternoon.

"I'm glad to see you, Doctor Berkowitz. Grace, this is the doctor who has come to see Stephen. Doctor, this is my wife, Grace."

"I'm glad to meet you, Doctor Berkowitz. And thank you so much—more than we can say—for your kindness in looking in on Stephen."

"Actually, it would be much better if I could see him at the medical center. But that would obviously involve impossible risk. So we'll just have to make the best of the situation here. In a way, I feel like a medical anachronism, making a patient call in the home. Remember that old picture you still sometimes see of a doctor a century ago, sitting at a child's bed at night, with his chin in his hand? That's me, tonight."

Grace smiled. Jon trusted his wife's judgment and was relieved to see that she liked Doctor Berkowitz.

"Now, where's the patient?"

"In his bedroom. Follow me." Jon went up the stairs.

"Don't tell him my name. There's no reason to take more of a risk than necessary. What he doesn't know, he can't reveal."

"I won't," Jon agreed.

They entered the bedroom, where the wallscreen was colorful

with a television program—a teacher was printing words on a lightboard for a class of first graders.

"Stephen obviously can't go to school, so we access his class. Since he usually feels better at night, though he didn't last night, we delay school until then. —Stephen, we brought a friend up to see you, and to look at your leg. This man is a doctor; he's going to try to make it better. Doctor, this is Stephen."

"Hi, Stephen. Do you like learning to read? I'll bet you miss seeing the kids at school each day. Let's take a look at that leg. First, I'll pull your pajamas down. Do the boys and girls in your class ever say anything to you, do they wave at you, when the class is televised? Probably not, I guess, since your class met earlier today and it's stored in the computer." —But, as if in answer, a girl on the first row spoke softly, "Hi, Steve." The teacher turned from the lightboard and said, "That will be enough of that. But we are glad you're with us, Stephen, even though we can't see you, and you may not see us until later. We hope you're soon back in class."

Jon went to the wall panel and turned off the computer television.

All the while he was speaking, the doctor was feeling Stephen's leg, especially in the area of the hip. His touch was gentle; yet at one point Stephen cried out.

"Ah, we have it. Yes, there's a pretty big hematoma here; mind if I move your leg? It'll hurt some." Stephen began to cry as he bent the leg at the hip.

"Hip socket's involved some, but it would be surprising if it weren't. Now, let me hear you breathe. This won't hurt." He took a stethoscope out of the shopping bag. Holding it up, he turned to Jon and Grace. "With the sophisticated equipment at the medical center, I've almost forgotten how to use one of these things."

He listened, moving the instrument about on Stephen's chest and back. "I want to make sure, with all this lying around he's been doing, that there's no other problem. No, it sounds all right. Perfectly healthy, except for that leg.

"Now," he continued, speaking to Stephen, "I'm going to give you some new blood that will help your leg begin to heal. It doesn't look like blood—" he reached into the shopping bag and brought out a plastic bag—"because it doesn't have everything in it. It's called plasma, and what it does have in it is exactly what your leg needs." He unwound a plastic tube.

"Could you bring a floor lamp or something I can hang this from?"

Jon soon returned with a lamp.

"Good. Now this will hurt you some, and you'll have to lie very still—but it will help you get well so you can begin to play outside again, and return to school. All right?"

"Yes, I'll try not to cry," Stephen said.

"Cry all you want to. Just don't move your arm. Now let's see—that looks pretty good. First I'll wash it off with alcohol. It has to be good and clean, so we kill all the bugs—"

"Bugs?" Stephen looked puzzled. "There aren't any bugs on my arm."

Price Berkowitz laughed, a free, hearty laugh. "Not bugs, but things called bacteria—I just call them bugs. Now I'm going to stick in this needle—hold very still, just like—that." He turned a small valve. The plasma began to drip out of the bottle, through the tube, into Stephen's arm.

"You didn't cry."

"It didn't hurt at all, almost."

"Now you can go to sleep—no more school for tonight. I'm pleased I still remember how to insert a needle. The R.N.'s always do it at the hospital." Then he turned to Jon and Grace, "I'll stay awhile, just to make sure everything's going all right."

Stephen closed his eyes. The three adults were silent, allowing him to go to sleep. The silence was warm; it was almost as if they were embracing one another.

They heard other sounds outside the room: a siren in the distance, a supersonic plane's roar overhead, cars in the street and a subway train's rumble. But the room itself was still. A small light recessed in the ceiling cast a dim glow. The plasma

36

dripped, one drop at a time, through the transparent plastic tube.

Doctor Berkowitz broke the silence, speaking in a low voice. "Well, I guess that will keep going for another hour or so. One of you will have to sit up here until it stops—just to make sure he doesn't turn over suddenly and pull out the needle. When the bottle is almost empty, close this little valve at the top of the tube—turn it down, this way—and then pull the needle straight out. Don't be afraid you'll hurt anything."

He reached into the shopping bag once more. "Here's a self-adhesive bandage to put over the place where the needle entered. Put a fair amount of pressure on it with your finger when you first put it on, for five or ten minutes. Then go to bed and forget about it."

"What will the plasma do?" Jon asked.

"It will temporarily raise the coagulation level of the blood. We'll hope that hip begins to heal then, that the bleeding—or oozing of blood inside—stops so it can heal. At any rate, I'll be back tomorrow night."

"When will Stephen's leg be well?"

"I hope after a few more transfusions."

Grace said, "I'll stay here with Stephen; you take Doctor Berkowitz to the door, Jon." She took Doctor Berkowitz's hand. "Thank you, doctor. I admire your courage."

"I admire it myself. Maybe I'm just trying to prove that there's some left. For that matter, you two people seem to have a rather large measure of it. Good night, Mrs. Stanton."

At the door to the street, Jon shook the doctor's hand. "Will you be here about the same time tomorrow night?"

"Yes, just about. Now you know I can't promise that this will do the trick. We may be too late to prevent some damage to the hip. But at least we can prevent further damage, and help it heal."

"Yes, I know. And thanks."

The next night Price Berkowitz returned and repeated the procedure, and again the following night. The second night he only talked for several minutes with Grace and Jon, but this time he stayed for more than an hour while the plasma was being transfused.

In a thoughtful way, while standing beside Stephen's bed, talking more to himself than to Jon and Grace, the doctor said, "I wish I could transfuse something into my son that would change his condition."

"You can't do anything?" Grace asked.

"No, it's—hopeless. Tay-Sachs involves progressive deterioration, physical and mental. Death usually occurs around age three or four. In the meantime, we can only provide loving care. A warm nest."

"How's your wife taking it?"

"Hard. She cries a lot, and has gotten into alcohol. I can't say I blame her. But it sort of complicates things at home."

"Do you have any other children?"

"Are you kidding? Even doctors are limited to one. Zero-minus population growth for us too. Only the politicians, the models for society, seem to be able to wangle a permit for more than one."

"I hope you've combed yourself. This room is clean, and so are we, but—"

"I do every time I come here. It's not just political heresy we have to be worried about. That's all we need, to be found out in this foul deed: saving the life of a child. We'd all be sent to a detention camp. And as for Stephen . . ."

"How could this ever happen?"

"I've tried to figure that out. It seems to me that a certain point of no return was passed in the early seventies, when the Supreme Court made abortion legal for any cause or none. I'm not blaming the Court—things had been heading up that way anyway. Then when people got accustomed to aborting a fetus, even a viable one, the medical researchers said, 'Look, why do we have to kill those babies? Why not use them for experiments?' At first there was an outcry, people—including some physicians—said it was immoral. But then pragmatism won the battle, as it always does. If a fetus can be torn to pieces, why

38

can't an aborted fetus, a viable one, be kept alive and used in experiments, the same as rats and dogs and little pigs?"

"You make it sound so natural," Grace said.

"That's the way it seemed at the time. After that, it was just another logical step to destroy newborn infants, normally born ones that were found to have congenital problems. Why should parents or the government spend money on their care? It was maybe five years later that someone had the great idea of the organ factory.

"Can't you see it? This whole country's cursed. Jews and Wasps, Blacks, Chicanos, everybody. It's cursed with health and intelligence and beauty. Everyone's so damned beautiful, so damned bright, so damned healthy."

He stood up. "But I've got to go. I'd have a hard time explaining what I'm doing on the street so late at night, if they stopped me. Especially with this." He tapped the stethoscope in his pocket.

They watched him from the window as he walked rapidly toward the subway, watched until he turned the corner.

"A brave man," Jon said as they turned away from the window.

"A truly beautiful person."

THE NEXT afternoon Price called Jon to say that he couldn't come that night. "Something has come up here at home—" His voice trailed off. "But anyway, the deal is going through and one day won't make any difference. Just see that . . . the papers aren't disturbed."

"Let's ask mother and dad to come over," Grace suggested, after Jon had explained that Price wouldn't be coming. "They'll be thrilled to see how much better Stephen is."

The parents came early in the evening. George Duncan was retired; he and his wife Jean led an active life, traveling, gardening, and had many friends.

Tonight George wasn't his usual self. He only seemed to want to hold Stephen on his lap, not taking part in the conversation around him. The little talking he did was with his grandson.

Jean was unusually quiet, too.

After Stephen was in bed, Grace asked them what was wrong.

"What's the matter, dad? You seem depressed—mom, too. If it's about Stephen, I really think God has answered prayer, the prayers of all of us."

"No, it's not Stephen," her father answered. "We're as thrilled as you are about how he's improved. You know I've just had my seventy-fifth birthday."

"That means . . . you got your termination notice, didn't you? Oh, dad, they can't terminate you. You're too well, and too strong, and—" She paused, "and vital."

"They can, and they're going to. Come December twenty-second. Or at least they think they're going to."

"Only three months?" Her voice was agitated. "That's awful." She got up from the couch, went over, threw her arms around his neck and kissed him. Then she returned to her seat on the couch beside her mother.

"Don't start crying for me yet," he said with sudden resolve. "I may still have some tricks up my sleeve."

"When we talked about it a couple of years ago," Jon said, "you said you were ready to die at any moment, that you weren't uptight about the prospect."

"That was just before his heart transplant. That was when God might have taken him naturally, not the government," Grace said.

"Grace . . ." Her mother looked troubled.

"I guess that's the point." George stood and punched a fist into his open palm for emphasis. "That way would have been

40

natural, if transplants are natural—sometimes I wonder even about that. But this isn't natural. It's not the way God planned things, to have men kill other men because of their age. I'm not afraid to die, but I'd like it to come as a surprise—like when I used to travel a lot, before I retired, and I'd be away a couple of weeks at a time. Sometimes I'd come back to the hotel after dinner, stop for the key, and the clerk would hand me a letter with Jean's handwriting on it."

"Not often enough, I'm afraid," Jean said quietly.

"That's not the point," George continued. "I didn't write home to you, either. But there'd be this letter, and she'd say something like, 'I love you, and I miss you, so why not cut your trip short and come home? The business will take care of itself.' That's what I'd like God to say. Instead, some bureaucrat sends me a form letter, 'Report to the thanotel on December twenty-second by seven p.m. The dinner and beverages of your choice will be served, and you will be terminated at eleven p.m.'"

They were all completely silent. Just as the silence began to become oppressive, Jon asked, "Would you really rather die of one of the old diseases—cancer, a paralyzing stroke, a heart attack—than be put to sleep in the thanotel? Or spend months or even years in one of those horrible nursing homes like they had in your parents' day?"

"Are those the only options? It seems to me that a lot of people died while they were sitting on the toilet in those days, or shoveling snow, or just eating at the table, surrounded by their families. This management of death—it's an awful thing. Death no longer means anything, it's the same for everyone. You get to be seventy-five, and you get your expiration notice. Like the old days, when a library book was overdue, or a bill that you owe."

"How do you feel about it, mother?" Grace laid her hand on her mother's hand, felt the wedding band underneath.

"I wish I were six years older, so we'd get our notices at the same time. I can't bear to think of waiting all those days and weeks and months . . . without George."

"Do you know what I think I'll do?" George asked in a strong, determined manner.

"What?"

"I'll kill myself just before the day I'm supposed to show up at the thanotel. At least they won't have the satisfaction of putting me to sleep."

"You can't. That's suicide, dad. Only people like Judas, or Saul, committed suicide."

"Don't worry," he said, "I don't guess I'll do it. Not that I don't have the nerve. Or that I think it's wrong. It's not any more wrong for me to kill myself than for them to murder me. At least it's my own body."

Jon answered. "The difference between the two situations is that the government does it in one case, and you—a private citizen, a man who believes in Jesus, do it in the other. God has put the government over us for us to obey."

"Now I've got you." His tone was triumphant. "Why didn't you and Grace give in to the government when it came to—"

"Because that was wrong. The government has no business taking a child and treating him like a machine to be recalled, an object."

"Then why isn't it just as wrong for the government to treat me like a library book, to tell me my time is up?"

Grace hurried to speak. "It is wrong. Terribly wrong."

"Yes, you're right," Jon said. "But when the government does it, when the Congress and courts agree to it, what can people like us do?"

"Dear, I think we should be getting home." Jean spoke in a hopeless manner. "Tomorrow is another day."

"Yes, tomorrow is—let's see, it's— Tonight's September fifteenth, and there are thirty days in September, thirty-one in October, thirty in November, and on December twenty-second. . . . Tomorrow is exactly one ninety-eighth of the rest of my life." He rose to go. "From here on in, even the minutes are precious."

"Will you come over for dinner with us Saturday night?" She hugged her father. "Please."

"Of course. You didn't think we'd just hibernate for the next ninety-eight days, did you? We'll be here pestering you more than ever. Especially since you have Stephen, our grandson." He kissed Grace.

Price Berkowitz came on Friday night and was pleased with Stephen's progress. He moved the injured leg back and forth, touched the hip in various places, before he said, "I think tonight's plasma will be the last. There's no pain, and the hematoma has definitely gone down, it's softer."

While the plasma was slowly dripping in through the needle in Stephen's arm, Grace talked about her parents. "They were here last night. But they weren't their usual selves. Dad has just received his termination notice and they were sort of despairing."

"He's seventy-five, then. How's his health?"

"Great," Jon replied. "He's more active than I am. But, dear," he said, turning to Grace, "despair is too strong a word. It was more of a mild depression. Mixed with bitterness."

"Despair, depression, bitterness—what difference does it make? He's a human being, and they're treating him like an animal, or a computer that's been superseded by a new model, a new generation. Pull the plug, send it to the junkyard."

"I guess it's another of those things you don't think about until it strikes someone close to you," Grace said. "Then it's too late to do anything except complain. And get bitter."

"You know," Price said, "we've come to accept termination, or at least most people have. We're in danger of forgetting those first six months after it began. They're a blot on America and American medicine that we'll never outlive. Six million elderly people were killed. The same number of Jews died in Hitler's holocaust. You remember how the United Nations even got into it, on a formal complaint joined by Russia and China. My grandparents were included. What a terrible irony—my grandfather came out of Auschwitz alive as a young man, only to be executed at age eighty-one in Brooklyn. Not in a gas chamber, but in a thanotel."

"My father says he's going to commit suicide the day before

he's supposed to report to the thanotel." Grace was crying now; the conversation, coupled with her concern over Stephen, was beginning to tell.

"Hooray for him. I can see where you get your courage, Grace." Their shared concern for Stephen had put the three on a first-name basis, even though they had known each other for less than a week.

Grace objected. "But it would be wrong. Suicide is never right."

"It would be wrong, that's for sure," Price agreed. "But which is worse, suicide or murder?"

Jon answered, "They're both against the law—the law of the state, and God's law in the Bible."

"But if the state kills Grace's father, it's not murder?"

"No," Jon said, "God has given the power of the sword to our rulers."

"The sword? That's strange language."

"Jon means that our rulers are responsible to God when they kill someone; in war, for instance. We don't question it. It's not murder."

"The state can kill and it's not murder?" Price's tone was unbelieving. "You don't question the state's right to order your father to report to the thanotel and put him to death? I can't believe it." He shook his head.

"Uh, well, the Apostle Paul was the one who said that. He said it in the first century, when he wrote to the Christian community in Rome," Jon explained.

"If he did, he was simply giving his own opinion. He couldn't have had God behind what he said. Otherwise there's no difference between God and the devil. We wouldn't need to worry about being bugged on this conversation—you're saying exactly what they want to hear. A long time ago, Thoreau said he refused to surrender his conscience to the state. But you've done it. Not with Stephen, which puzzles me, but with your father. I've already said too much, but I'll say one thing more before I go: I've always been puzzled over the silence of the

44

church in Germany when Hitler went raging after the Jews and killing them. For the first time, I think I understand it. The Christians thought Hitler was God's gun, or God's sword as you put it. So they didn't have to object to what he did. Their consciences weren't disturbed because they were resting in Hitler's pocket. What a sick religion."

"That's wrong. You don't understand," Jon said.

"I hope I don't, but I'm afraid I do. Now I must take that needle out and leave. I'll be back again tomorrow night, just to check. I don't think he'll need any more plasma—now it's just a matter of waiting a few days and then gradually getting that leg back into action. We'll hope that there won't be any permanent effects from the injury. Kids are great that way—they're more likely to snap right back than adults are. Maybe they don't know they can't, so they do."

BY SATURDAY afternoon Stephen was walking short distances inside the house. Doctor Berkowitz wanted him to exercise his leg, to try to get the hip working smoothly again. The limp that had been so noticeable at first began to disappear.

Joy pervaded the household.

Grace hummed to herself as she worked in the kitchen, following a recipe printed out by the videotext. Jon, home from work for the weekend, helped Stephen walk around the house. In the afternoon, Grace and Jon sat on the couch with Stephen between them. He hadn't been out of his room for more than a week.

45

Grace's parents came for dinner on Saturday evening. Even they were affected by the happy mood. Their eyes never left Stephen when he walked about the downstairs area.

The dinner was festive. "I'm going to celebrate by having an old-fashioned formal table setting," Grace announced. "Mother and dad will like that." And so she brought out the china and sterling silver, had candles and a low arrangement of asters in the center of the white linen tablecloth.

"This steak is sure good," George Duncan said. "Done just right. I don't know when I've enjoyed a meal so much."

"Me too," Jean agreed.

"How about you, Stephen? Do you want me to cut your meat? Here, hand it over. . . . This doctor must be some man."

"He is," Grace agreed enthusiastically. "You'll really like him."

"Why—are we going to meet him?"

"Yes, he's coming over this evening. He wants to take one final look at Stephen's leg. And we wanted you to become acquainted with him."

"I can't say I'm too anxious to meet any doctor now," her father said, his face suddenly old. "I'll be seeing my last one ninety-five days from now. In fact, I'll just be checking in at the thanotel about this time. If I do check in."

"Let's not talk about that tonight, dear," his wife said. "We don't want to put a damper on the happiness here by bringing up our troubles." She squeezed his hand.

The doorbell rang. Grace looked at the scanner, then opened the door. "Price—we're so glad to see you. . . . Come here, Stephen. See, he walks almost as well as if it had never happened. Say hello to your doctor, Stephen."

"Hi. Can I start to ride my bike again?"

"Not for a few more days, Stephen. And then you'd better try running first, rather than riding your bike. But your mother will tell you what you can do when that time comes."

"Hello, doctor. Looks pretty good, doesn't he?" Jon rose from his chair as the doctor entered the dining room with Grace.

"I'll say he does." He looked at the table. "Sorry to be interrupting your meal."

"That's all right. Have you eaten?"

"Yes, just finished. But I'll have some coffee with you."

"Mother and father, this is the doctor we've been telling you about." Grace put her hands on the Duncans' shoulders as she stood behind them and faced him. "We owe him a great deal, as we've told you."

"We sure do," George said. "I'm glad to meet you, doctor." He grasped Price's hand. "You've got guts."

"Someone had to step in and help." Price spoke self-deprecatingly. "So even though my field isn't hematology . . . Stephen, do you want to come into the kitchen with your father and me? I want to take one last look at that leg."

They left the room, and came back a few minutes later. "Looks great. Swelling has almost disappeared. He can go back to school next week—provided there isn't much of a limp. No sense in alerting the authorities at this point. They might ask questions."

"I won't limp, doctor. I promise not to."

"Good boy. But sometimes a person can't help limping. So we'll let your mother decide on Monday."

Jon brought a chair to the table, placing it between himself and Grace. "Here, Price, sit down. Have some coffee—and some of this fabulous dessert. Grace's mother made it."

After they had finished, Jon brought a Bible from the living room. "Each night we read something from the Bible before Stephen goes to bed," he explained to Price. "Then we pray. Right now we're about halfway through Jeremiah, the weeping prophet."

"The one who told his own people that God would punish them for their injustices?" Price asked.

"That's right. Send them into captivity."

"We Jews have no prophets today, not a single one of them. Just rabbis who say what the government—or we ourselves— want them to say, or don't mind them saying. Are there any Christian prophets? Do you have any?"

47

"No, I guess not," Jon replied. "Maybe a few in the black church. Then there's a group I've heard of called Sojourners, but they've pretty well isolated themselves. They live in monastic communities."

Price turned and asked George, "Why was Jeremiah called 'the weeping prophet'? Was it because he was suffering with his people, or because his people hated him and wanted to do away with him?"

"I don't know."

"It doesn't really make much difference, I guess," Price answered his own question.

"You seem to know the Bible pretty well," George Duncan said.

"'For a Jew.' That's what you meant, wasn't it?" Price laughed. "You're right in being surprised. Most Jews don't, but I had a strict orthodox upbringing. Hebrew school and all the rest. I do know the Bible, the Jewish Bible. And I cherish it. — But Jon, I've interrupted your reading. Please go on."

Jon read a chapter, then closed the Bible.

"Whoever wants to can pray," he said.

"Dear Jesus," Stephen began, "thank you for helping my doctor make my leg well. Thanks that nana and grandpa could come. Amen."

George Duncan and Jon also prayed.

"Off to bed, Stephen." Grace led the way upstairs. "Kiss grandma and grandpa and then come on."

"I've come to have a lot of respect for your daughter and son-in-law," Price said to the older people while Grace was putting Stephen in bed. "I might even make that stronger and say affection."

"And we toward you," Jon quickly responded.

"Not that we agree on everything. Like the other night, they tried to tell me that whatever the state does is God's will, and those who want to please God must obey the state. Have I said it right, Jon?"

"Not quite. It's not that everything our rulers do is right—far

48

from it. But their power comes from God, and so we must obey them."

"All right. That's close enough. —How do you feel about that, sir?" He turned toward Grace's father.

"Substantially the same as Jon, at least as he expressed it just now."

"I gather that this is said in your Bible?"

"Yes, the Apostle Paul wrote this to the Roman Christians. But it's in your Bible, too, in the Old Testament. God was considered the source of all authority, so people obeyed their rulers because their authority came from God—that is, people did if they knew him."

"How about Moses' mother and the midwives? Seems to me they didn't exactly obey the Egyptian rulers when they said boy babies were to be put to death."

Jon was quick to reply. "Moses' mother actually did obey the rulers when she put him out on the water, in the little ark. Only she didn't drown him."

Grace returned to the room.

"That's pure rationalization to prove your point. The midwives and Moses' mother, and everyone else who was involved, did everything they could to keep that little boy from being killed. The same as you and I with Stephen. And it's good for us Jews—and Christians, too—that they did. When the state, whether it's Egypt or Germany or the United States, commands something that's against God's law—like killing Jews, or killing babies or old people—we've got to resist. Otherwise we're part of the conspiracy."

"Do you feel that way about old people, too?" Grace's father asked the question.

"I sure do. Termination is just the same as the organ factory. Both are wrong—the state has no more right to kill the old than it does to harvest children."

"See—that's what I've been telling you." Grace's father turned to face his wife and daughter, his face flushed, his voice agitated.

49

"But two wrongs don't make a right. The government's wrong act in terminating people at seventy-five doesn't make suicide right." Grace spoke quietly but firmly.

"Have you ever thought of running away, instead of committing suicide?" Price asked the question.

"Not really. Where could I run to? I'd need to show my identity card a couple of times the first day. And the computer check would show me scheduled for termination."

"Not right away—they wouldn't enter it in the computer until a few weeks before you were due at the thanotel. So you'd be safe until then. Have you received your notice yet?"

"Yes," replied Grace's father. "I'm due to report in ninety days."

"Then you still have time. As to where, why not Russia? You and your wife could apply for a passport and visa, then ask for asylum on humanitarian grounds. They'd doubtless grant it."

"But Russia's a communist country," Jon objected. "No Christian would think of emigrating there."

"And no Jew, ordinarily." Price paused for a moment. "But these are not ordinary times. And the question seems to be whether Grace's parents prefer to live in a communist country or be killed by a democracy. It's as simple as that, isn't it?"

Jon was silent. When he spoke, it was with strong conviction in his voice. "I don't think a Christian should ever think of going from the United States, bad as it may be, to Russia, or to any other communist country, for that matter. Why, it wouldn't—"

"Now wait a minute," Price interrupted. "You talk as if the United States was God's own special country, and everything about it is good, while everything about Russia is bad. But the very problem your father is trying to escape—his murder by the state—is found right here, and not in Russia. For that matter, your Stephen would be able to live a normal life in Russia instead of being marked for the organ factory if he's ever found out."

Grace's mother stood up and walked over to her daughter. "I think we had better be going home, dear. Good night, doctor.

Thank you from the bottom of our heart for your willingness to help our grandson and our children. And thank you for your concern for Grace's father and me. The fact that we do not follow your advice doesn't lessen our appreciation."

"I know that, Mrs. Duncan. It wasn't really advice, though, it was just a possible alternative to a losing situation. I can't say for sure that I'd take it myself if I were in your husband's place."

Price didn't stay long after the others had left. As he stood at the door, he said, "Look, this isn't any of my business, but I'm going to say it anyway. Everyone needs hope. Even old people. When you remove hope, you kill them just as surely as the state does at the thanotel."

"My parents have hope." Grace spoke in an intense voice. "Neither we, nor anyone else can take it from them. That's the hope of heaven, of the resurrection some day."

"I know that, or I assumed it." Any spirit of argument had left Price's voice. He spoke quietly. "But they need hope here and now, too. They need hope that they'll be alive and enjoying each other five years from now—ninety-one days from now, for that matter. Don't you see that?"

"I do," Grace said. "At least, I think I do."

"I've cared for Christians, and Jews, who had vast resources of faith in God and the hereafter. Not many, but some among all my patients. And do you want to know something? They struggled to live just as much as the pagans and agnostics. No difference. That, and the need for hope, is built into us. Into your parents, Grace."

"Maybe you're right," Jon half agreed. "But for George, to be absent from the body is to be present with the Lord. So what's the difference between ninety days and five or ten years?"

"Do you think it's easy for him to think of leaving Grace's mother, of her having to fend for herself? Remember, he's an active, healthy man—not an invalid, suffering, who might be reconciled to death. And to leave Grace and Stephen? You're losing your father-in-law, Grace is losing her father, Stephen's losing his grandfather, Grace's mother is losing her husband.

But George is losing wife, daughter, grandson, friends—everybody who means anything to him. Everybody, not just one person, like you. Small wonder he's depressed."

"Still, you shouldn't have encouraged his crazy ideas," Grace said.

"I know. I'm sorry, Grace. I must leave. Don't let Stephen go back to school on Monday if he has the slightest limp."

"I won't," Grace said as they walked with Price to the door.

STEPHEN STILL limped on Monday, and it was Thursday before he returned to school.

His mother warned, "You can go to school today, but don't say anything about the doctor coming here and taking care of your leg, dear. That's a secret, not to be told to anyone. Not anyone, even your friends or Ms. Pritchard. Do you understand, Stephen?"

"Sure, mom. I know how to keep a secret."

"Stevie, make sure you don't run and play rough during recess or after school, so you don't hurt your leg again. Now put on your coat. You don't want to miss the bus."

After Stephen left for school, Grace cleared the table and loaded dishes and utensils into the dishwasher. Then she decided to work outside. Today would be a good day to begin to prepare the roses and other perennials for winter, she thought. Not that a frost was expected, but the September weather had combined with a momentary return of summer's heat to make the day especially beautiful. And working in a garden cleared her mind, brought things into perspective.

She got her gardening basket and went outside, planning her work. The rose bushes needed to be cut back some and banked with dirt so they wouldn't be killed by winter. Gardening was one job that couldn't be trusted to computers and machines. Plants were too fragile to be treated like plastic dishes which could be dumped into the dishwasher without being damaged.

The trouble was that government treated people like plastic dishes, not like fragile plants and beautiful flowers. Of course, a lot of people were plastic, but there were gentle, sensitive ones, too. Like Price.

How good of God to take care of Stephen's bleeding incident the way he had. And to bring Price Berkowitz into their life, someone they wouldn't be afraid to turn to in the future. She had no doubt that they would need him for Stephen more than just this time. But now she could relax just a bit. Not relax in reminding Stephen to be careful, to avoid risks and bodily contact sports. That would always worry her. But still relax just a bit, knowing that Price would be there if something happened.

Her father and mother. They would be thrilled to know that Stephen was back in school, but what a burden they still carried, with his termination scheduled before Christmas. She mustn't let her joy over Stephen interfere with her grief for them. All those years together, suddenly brought to an end. There was scant comfort in the fact that the separation would be only temporary.

All the while, she was using her shears to cut back the branches, her trowel to build up a mound of dirt around the rosebushes. She noticed dead leaves from the trees covering the ground, but decided to wait several weeks until more had fallen to vacuum them up.

Everything faded and died like the flowers, the grass of the field, the grass she was kneeling on; everybody died. Her father—even if there were no such thing as termination—her mother, she herself and Jon. Stephen, too, although she hoped he would live to old age. But then . . . .

Being a Christian made a difference. She didn't know how other people faced the future without hope—hope of heaven, hope of Jesus coming back to earth, hope of the resurrection.

Why before Christmas, though? It was an awful and incomprehensible thing to happen at all, but especially right before the wonderful holiday . . . to have her father's termination date then.

What should she have for dinner? What would Jon like? It was funny—during the previous week, before Stephen began to get better, they had hardly cared what they ate, or whether. Now it was subtly, slightly different. They were beginning to take hold of life again, enjoy it. In spite of knowing about her father and mother.

So soon do people fall back to sleep after being awakened by a storm, she thought, and feel secure after the thunder and lightning have passed.

The phone rang.

Grace took off her gardening gloves as she hurried back into the house. She hoped whoever it was wouldn't hang up before she reached it.

When she touched the receiver button, Ruth Swanson's face appeared on the videoscreen.

"Good morning, Grace. I hope I didn't bring you from something important. You look out of breath."

"I was just working in the garden. And it was about time for some coffee anyway."

"How about if you wait until I come over, and we can have a cup together—that is, if you can spare the time for a little visit. I've been thinking about you, and thought I'd call you."

"That sounds great. I'll put the coffee on so it'll be ready when you get here."

"See you soon."

Grace was genuinely glad to see Ruth when she arrived twenty minutes later, even though she didn't know her well. After they had begun to drink their coffee, Ruth said, "I've been wanting to know about Stephen. How is he?"

"He's back in school today. Thanks so much for being concerned. Jon and I really appreciated your visit, with Norm, two Sundays ago."

54

"Did his hip injury just clear up by itself?"

"No, he had some help . . . although I'm afraid I can't tell you the source of the help. If I did, it would make you a sort of co-conspirator." She said it lightly, with a little laugh, but Ruth understood her seriousness.

"I'm so glad. And thankful that God answered prayer, however he did it."

"He did it completely out of the blue, I can say that much."

"We'd still like you to visit our little house church. We've told some of the sisters and brothers about you, and they—"

"Not about Stephen?" Grace's alarm was apparent. "You didn't tell them about his hemophilia, did you?"

"Well, no. But we did tell them that Stephen has a health problem we wanted them to pray about. That's not unusual—a lot of people have health problems and get prayed for. Anyway, they hope you'll visit our little group some Sunday night."

"Well, thank you, perhaps we will."

"And if you want us to anoint Stephen for healing, complete healing"—she emphasized the word *complete*—"we'll be glad to do this. Of course, you and Jon would have to believe God for this—believe that he will heal Stephen. Not just that he has the power to heal, but that he will heal. 'He that doubteth,' you know."

"I'll talk to Jon about it. Would you like another cup of coffee?"

"Yes, thank you, but I'll have to go soon."

Grace refilled both cups.

"How are your children, Ruth? You have two, don't you?"

"Yes we do. The minus-zero controls didn't start until after they were born, praise the Lord. Martha is thirteen, young Norman is sixteen. They're healthy, but . . . they don't seem to have much of an appetite for spiritual things. In fact, they're getting caught up in the world, especially Norman. Drinking, some drugs too, I think—although I have no proof. These are hard days for raising children."

"They certainly are. By the way, do they attend your house church?"

"No, they don't."

"I'm sorry."

"Well, give them time. I really must be going. I'm so glad Stephen's better."

After she had seen her visitor to the door, Grace put her gardening gloves on again.

As she thought of Ruth's visit, she wondered which she would choose: a child who would live to old age, and be eternally lost; or a child who would die at an early age, and go to be with Jesus? She frowned. Foolish alternatives—neither had to be true. She'd choose a child who would serve God all his life and die in old age.

If she had a choice. But the choice wasn't theirs.

"LET'S GO down to the shore for the weekend," Grace suggested when Jon arrived home from work the Thursday Stephen started back to school. "It would be nice for Stephen to be at a place where he could be entertained for a few days without wanting to ride his bike. Mother told me that she and dad were at the cottage several weeks ago, a few days before he got his termination notice. They haven't felt like going back since."

"Maybe they'd go down with us," Jon suggested. "It would probably do them good, as well as Stephen. We could help them close the place up for the winter. Besides, it would be nice to have one last fling at Cape May."

"I'll ask." But Grace's parents did not want to go.

"How about asking Price and his wife? And their little boy?"

"Sounds great," Jon said. "I'll call him."

Price agreed at once. "But we won't bring young Price along—my mother is happy to keep him for us." He paused. "One other thing, I can't promise that Linda won't be . . . sick."

"We understand," Jon quickly replied. "How about leaving early Friday morning, to avoid the heavy traffic?"

"Sorry, Jon, I should have told you I can't leave until late Friday afternoon. I'll be at the hospital all day. If that makes any difference in your plans—"

"It doesn't. Now tell me where we can pick you and Linda up. At your apartment, or at the hospital?"

"I'll drive. And we'll stop for you—around seven o'clock, after supper. Is that all right?"

Jon and Grace were ready by six-thirty on Friday night, their bags by the door, and Stephen was getting restless. They weren't surprised that Price and Linda hadn't come by seven; things often turned up to delay people, and this must be particularly true of a doctor. At eight, they began to be concerned, since Price had neither come nor called on the phone.

"I think I'll call him," Jon said at nine o'clock. But the call was unanswered.

"We'd better put Stephen to bed," Grace suggested. "We can always get him up and ready in a few minutes when Price and Linda do get here."

"I hope nothing has happened. He isn't the sort of person to forget. He'd call if he couldn't make it."

At ten o'clock, again failing to get an answer at Price's home phone, Jon said, "I think I'll call the hospital and try to contact him there."

He spoke the hospital's name into the phone.

"Federal Hospital," a woman's voice answered.

"Doctor Price Berkowitz, please."

"Will you repeat that name, and tell me who is calling?"

"Doctor Price Berkowitz."

"We have no doctor registered by that name. Now give me your name."

Jon quickly replaced the phone.

Grace saw that he was disturbed. "What's the matter, dear?"

"The woman at the hospital says that they have no doctor named Price Berkowitz. Something must be wrong, terribly `wrong. She wanted my name, but I hung up. I'm only glad she didn't ask for my name first."

"What could have happened?"

"I'm afraid to even guess."

Early the next morning, Jon called Price's home phone. After many rings, a woman's voice answered. But no image appeared on the videoscreen.

"Who do you want?"

"Doctor Price Berkowitz."

"I'm afraid he can't be reached."

"Don't hang up for a moment, please. Is this his wife? I'm Jon Stanton."

"I don't recognize your name. Good-by."

"She sounded frightened," Jon said to Grace. "Really frightened. I wonder what's happened."

"Maybe you'd better not try to find out just now, especially since she was frightened enough not to want to admit that she knew your name."

"Provided she did know it. But I guess you're right. I'm afraid for Price. I surely hope helping us—Stephen—didn't get him in trouble."

A small item in Saturday morning's video-news printout explained what had happened. Jon tore it off the videotext and rushed into the laundry, where Grace was loading the sonic cleaner.

"Look at this."

She read the brief account aloud. "Surgeon Banished to Alaska: Price Berkowitz, M.D., general surgeon on the staff of Federal Hospital, this city, was arrested by agents of the FBI yesterday afternoon. At a subsequent trial before Federal Circuit Judge Matthew Kennelly, Berkowitz was convicted of violating a section of the American Medical Association-United States Department of Health code that prohibits treatment of unassigned patients. No details of the charge have been revealed. After the trial and conviction, which automatically excludes the surgeon from all professional practice, Berkowitz was sent on the midnight custodial flight to Alaska. Linda Berkowitz, wife of the convicted man, is unavailable for comment."

"Poor Price. And poor Linda. And whatever will become of young Price?"

"We'll have to find out about them and help them—if we can. I'll get on it as soon as I get to the office Monday morning."

"It might be safer for her—for us, too, for that matter—if I tried to find out instead of you," Grace said. "I'll look more like a friend of hers, and probably not draw as much attention to myself as you would."

"All right. You try to contact her, and I'll see if anything can be done as far as Price is concerned. But from what I've heard, that's just about hopeless."

"Nothing is hopeless. 'With God, all things are possible.'"

"Even bringing someone back from detention in Alaska?"

"Jon, don't make light of the power of God."

"I'm not making light of it. You'll try to find Linda, then?"

"Yes, I will."

Grace left for the Berkowitz's apartment soon after Stephen had gone to school the following Monday. When she got there, nobody came to the door, although she rang and knocked repeatedly.

Finally the door to the next apartment was opened, just a crack, and a woman's voice asked, "Were you looking for someone?"

"Yes—Linda Berkowitz. She's a friend of mine."

"She needs a friend right now," the woman said. "But I don't know where you'll find her. Besides, how do I know you're her friend and not a policewoman?"

"You don't, I guess. And you have no reason to trust me. But for that matter, I have no reason to trust you, either. So goodby. If you see Linda, tell her Grace called."

"Grace who?"

"Never mind."

"Oh—you're scared of the police, too. Well, try the Capricorn Tavern, over on Carter Boulevard. She spends a lot of time there."

"Thanks so much. I promise you, I'm her friend. I'd like to help her."

"Well, even if you're not, you can't hurt her much more than already she's been hurt, that's for sure. That great Doctor Berkowitz. That he should be sent from here, where he's helped so many people, to a prison camp in Alaska. If you're not her friend, you can go back to your damn bosses and tell them that Anna Shulker, age seventy-three, almost ready for their damn termination and so not afraid any more, almost, says that they are all sons of a mach. Don't forget it. They're all sons of a mach."

"I agree with you."

"If you do find Linda, tell her she's welcome at Anna Shulker's. I'll never forget when I was so sick last winter. . . ."

Grace walked over to Carter Boulevard and found the Capricorn Tavern in the second block. She hesitated several stores away. She had never been in a tavern, and the thought of breaking the pattern of a lifetime was vaguely disturbing. Besides, what if someone from the church should pass and see her go in?

Suddenly she was ashamed, thinking of the great risk Price had taken for her little boy. And couldn't she trust God to take care of her reputation? She hoped there wouldn't be men to heckle her, at least.

She went in.

When her eyes had adjusted to the darkness after the bright sunlight, she saw that there were only two people at the bar. One was a young woman. Grace sat down on the stool next to her.

"What'll it be?" asked the bartender.

"A glass of tomato juice, I guess."

"Bloody Mary?"

"No—just tomato juice, please."

"Virgin Mary coming up."

60

When he set it down in front of her, Grace paid him, took a sip, then turned to the young woman next to her.

"Excuse me for asking, but is your name Linda?"

The woman didn't answer.

"Don't bother her, lady," the bartender said. "She's got something on her mind and she doesn't want to talk to anyone."

"I'm her friend," Grace said. "That is, if she's Linda."

"If you were, I'd think she'd recognize you. But she doesn't. So don't bother her."

"Actually, she doesn't know me, so she doesn't know that I'm her friend."

"How can you be her friend if she doesn't know you?"

"What's your name?" The young woman looked up and spoke for the first time.

"Grace. Grace Stanton."

"Don't know anybody by that name. Now leave me alone."

"Yeah, lady, leave her alone." The man at the other end of the bar expressed his annoyance. "What did you come in here for anyway, with your tomato juice? Go on home."

Grace decided to try one last approach to the young woman. She spoke softly so that neither the bartender nor the other man could hear, moving her head next to the other woman's ear.

"My husband and I owe an awful lot to your—"

"Damn it, will you stop?" The young woman's eyes flashed fire.

Grace reluctantly left the tavern.

That night she told Jon what had happened.

"You went into a tavern?" he exclaimed. "You, Grace Duncan Stanton, actually entered the portals of a drinking place?" he laughed.

"Don't be funny. You would too, if you could do anything for Price Berkowitz."

"But what if someone had seen you?"

"God could have blinded them, or made them see someone else. Or for that matter, he might have wanted to humble me by letting the rumor get started that I'm a secret alcoholic, an early morning drinker."

"On line, Grace. Actually I'm not surprised at Linda's reaction, if that's who it was. How could she be sure that she could trust you? She may even blame us for what happened to him. The news story did say that he was convicted for treating patients who weren't assigned to him. That could be Stephen. And if it is, or if Price's wife thinks it is, you can't blame her for not wanting to have anything to do with us. If she weren't Price's wife, I'd be afraid she'd report us."

"But if it were Stephen they knew about, wouldn't the police have checked on us before now?"

"Not necessarily. Sometimes they take their time. Keep you hanging."

"What can we do about Linda? I feel guilty, if we had anything to do with Price's arrest. Or if she thinks we did."

"I don't think there's anything we can do at the present time. We can pray for her, but anything that would involve our contacting her right now would probably be dangerous to her—to us, too, if they have any information about Stephen. She apparently didn't want any contact, either."

"What about me?" The boy, unnoticed, had come into the room.

"Oh, it's nothing that concerns you," Jon answered.

"Maybe we should tell him," Grace said tentatively.

"I guess you're right. Stephen, the federal police picked up our friend, the doctor who looked after your leg. That's the reason he and his wife didn't show up when we were going to go to Cape May. They've sent him to a prison in Alaska."

"What did he do? Shoot somebody?"

"No, of course not." He paused, trying to decide how to help the child understand what had happened. "I guess you could say he was punished for trying to help people. Certainly he never hurt anyone."

"But my doctor was good," Stephen said. "He made my leg all right again."

"Yes, he was good."

"Then the police were bad to arrest him."

"No, they were just doing their duty."

"What's duty?"

"It's something you do because it's right to do it. You obey the people who are over you, like you do what mother and I tell you to do. In the case of the police, they obey their leader."

"Who is their leader, dad?"

"The President, I guess."

"Daddy, would the President tell the police to do something bad like that—arresting my doctor?"

"Of course she wouldn't, Stephen. Now it's time for supper."

"Supper isn't quite ready yet," Grace said, a little too quickly. "You can go on answering your son's questions."

"Who did tell them to do such a bad thing, daddy? Somebody must have."

"A law was passed in Congress, and when someone breaks that law, he has to be arrested."

"Daddy, what was that word I didn't know?"

"What word?"

"He means duty, dear."

"Yes, daddy. You said policemen have a duty. Do you have a duty?"

"Of course, I have all sorts of duties at the office, things I have to do for the company I work for."

"But I don't mean at your office. I mean, do you have a duty like the police?"

"I guess I do. Now let's have supper."

After Stephen was in bed, Jon picked up the conversation, with Grace. "Maybe I do have a duty, a duty to Price."

"What kind of duty?"

"I don't know. There isn't anything we can do as far as the authorities are concerned, I guess."

"Not without endangering Stephen. And we can't do that."

"That's the trouble—you're never free and unencumbered when it comes to this sort of thing. You've got a child to think about, or a wife, or your position to think of. They could take away everything. When you're really unencumbered—before you're married—you don't know enough about how things are done to use your freedom."

"I guess that's one reason the government does everything it can for the young."

"Yes, they learned that from the campus riots of the sixties. They never want that again. But to get back to my duty—"

"Do you really have any?"

"Maybe not to the government—it's impossible to do anything that will turn it around. Besides, I'm no Dietrich Bonhoeffer."

"Was he the German Christian who was in on the plot to kill Hitler?"

"Yes, and was hanged for it. I'm not built like him. But what's my duty to Linda, to Price himself? And to their little boy? Do I have any?"

Grace was silent.

"Why don't you suggest something? You must have some ideas about this whole thing," Jon asked.

"I think of things, but right away Stephen's face comes to my mind. I see him up there in bed, so helpless, so very helpless. Should you endanger him?" She began to cry.

"It's difficult. So very difficult. What does God want?" And in his mind, not aloud, "Or doesn't he care about a little boy like Stephen?"

Several days later Jon stopped at Linda Berkowitz's apartment on his way home from work. He rang the bell and waited a long time, looking steadily at the scanner lens.

Someone spoke from inside the door. "Who do you want?"

"Mrs. Berkowitz. I'm looking for Mrs. Linda Berkowitz. My name is Jon Stanton."

"Can't you people leave me alone? I just want to be left alone. You should see that by now."

"Wait a minute," Jon said, "please open the door. We just want to help you. If we did anything to hurt Price, we're terribly sorry. We probably can't do anything for him now, but we can for you . . . and your—"

"Come in," she said, opening the door. "You shouldn't be talking outside in the hall that way."

He went into the apartment. A large photograph of Price was set, almost defiantly, on a small stand facing the door. Beyond, the living room was decorated tastefully in shades of brown with small touches of orange.

"Sit down," Linda said. "That chair is comfortable. Price used to like it."

"You know who I am, then. You recognized my name."

"Yes, and I knew who your wife was at the tavern a few days ago. It's not just your name—I think I'd have known who you were even if you hadn't told me. Price talked a lot about you and Grace, and your little boy—Stephen, isn't it?—the last week or so. And Grace's parents. He was really impressed with your family."

"And we with him. He was—is—a great person."

"Yes, I have to remind myself that it's is rather than was. With him in Alaska, it seems as if I'll never see him again, as if he's already dead."

"But he's not. And you still have—"

"Price Junior? Is that supposed to be good? I lie awake at night waiting for the police to come for him, to take him to the thanotel and the organ factory."

"Do they know about him?"

"I don't know. For that matter, how did they know about Price—that he was treating patients who weren't on his list? The informer who told on him probably knew about our little boy, too."

Jon asked the question that had been at the front of his mind since he first learned of Price's arrest: "Do they know about Stephen, our boy, do they know that Price cared for him?"

"I don't know. I hope not, I sincerely hope not. But I don't know. At least your Stephen wasn't among the specific instances mentioned at the trial."

"Did Price have a lawyer?"

"Yes, but you know how they represent an ordinary citizen today—like the lawyers who represented Jews while Hitler was in power in Germany, or ordinary people in Russia. But at least he phoned me after the trial, before Price was flown out to Alaska. I hurried to the airport, but the prison plane had just left. So I didn't get to see him."

"It's devilish, how the government has speeded up trials, and cut out appeals."

"And no trial by jury in most federal cases. If Price could just

65

have been tried by the people he helped. He was a really loving man, a compassionate person."

"I know—nobody knows that better than Grace and I."

She began to cry.

His arms went around her. That's the way it was, he realized. To say he put his arms around her would not have been true. Many things are like that—your foot goes up at a curb, your eyes follow an attractive woman, your ears pick one particular voice out of a clamor.

His arms circled her protectively, drew her to him. And she came.

They stood silent for minutes.

"Thanks," she said. "I need to blow my nose." And she drew away from him, after a gentle momentary tightening of her arms around him.

Now he was uncertain. His arms, having acted, were now disturbingly awkward. He crossed them. Then he sat down on the couch; Linda sat next to him.

"What are you going to do?" He waited to ask the question until her hands had fallen from her face and crumpled the handkerchief into a ball.

"I have no idea. I guess I'll just continue my happy hour."

"You can't. Drink isn't an answer—it only adds to the problem."

"Does it?" Linda asked, her tone now bitter. "How do you know—have you ever been drunk, mindlessly drunk? Have you ever been drawn alone into an ugly black tunnel, smelling its death, deeply depressed, stumbling over almost corpses, falling on rocks that bruise and cut, other rocks falling on you, spiderwebs brushing your face, hearing the screams of the damned, though they aren't close enough to provide companionship—and joining in the screaming yourself? Have you? And then in the middle of the tunnel, or maybe it's just the beginning, you come into an open place—not really, but it seems like it's real—and you no longer hear the screams, you don't feel the rocks and spider webs, you don't feel anything, and there's light, temporary light, beautiful light. And you're no longer afraid. That's what drinking does for me."

"Until you come past that place and continue into the tunnel."

"Of course. But what's better, the endless tunnel, or a resting place in it? No light, or a little light? Feeling the rocks and webs, or not feeling anything at all? Being alone, or being with others who are just as alone as you are, and sharing your loneliness? Even a corpse finds company in a cemetery."

"I'm in a tunnel, too." He suddenly turned from her grief to his own. "My little boy is on his way to the organ factory."

"I know," Linda said. "But he isn't there yet—and where there's life, there's hope. You only see the signs, 'Tunnel ahead.' I'm in it—I smell the stench. And besides, you're not alone, even if you go into the tunnel—you have your wife. When you get deep in the tunnel, you can hold each other."

Jon shook his head. "Sometimes it doesn't work like that. Suffering doesn't automatically bring people together. A husband and wife can get separated from each other in the tunnel, become lost, so that they never come together again. That hasn't happened to Grace and me . . . yet. But it could. And I've seen it happen to others who seemed to love each other as much as we do."

"I know. I know. I still had Price when I started finding my own private refuges in the tunnel. The first time I got drunk was the night he told me that our little boy had Tay-Sachs disease. It was just a few days after our dear baby's second birthday. I didn't cling to Price, we didn't go to bed together—I cursed him, I spit in his face, and then I ran out of the house to a tavern and got drunk. That first happy hour lasted two days."

"It didn't solve anything."

"Nothing solves anything. Damn your moralizing," she shouted. Then she continued, her voice subdued, "Nothing solves it for you, either. When you step into that tunnel—when you leave your boy at the organ factory and know that you won't see him ever again—but he'll be there, staring vacantly at white walls, at sterile doctors and heartless nurses, losing a kidney here and a hand there—"

"Stop it." Jon stood up as he spoke. "This isn't helping you any more than it is me. You know I'm sorry—that's too mild a

67

word for it—for your little boy and for you. And for Price. And you know I'm aware of what will happen if our little boy goes to the organ factory. You don't need to rub it in for either of us."

"I'm sorry." She took his hand. "I didn't mean to—"

"I know. And I can't be sure that if our boy were taken to the organ factory I wouldn't begin to drink. I don't think I would, but— Why don't you come home with me? Grace will be glad to see you. And you wouldn't be alone."

"I'd be more alone there than I am here. But thanks."

The occasion was past, the warm moment of holding each other was ended, and both were back in their own separate tunnels. He still felt the pressure of her hand, now removed, on his own.

"I'll be going, then. I wish I could change your mind. If you want us, or if you decide to come visit us, just call on the phone. I'll come for you."

"Thanks. But I won't, or maybe I'd better say I don't think I will."

He paused at the door. "Grace and I will pray for Price and you, and for your little boy."

She was silent.

A SOFT knocking sound awakened Grace. She listened, then touched Jon's shoulder.

"Did you hear anything?"

He was instantly awake, straining to hear the sound. Again it came.

"Someone's at the door. I'll go," he said, as he got out of bed and put on his robe.

"I'll come too," Grace said, getting up. "I wonder who it is at this time of night." She was suddenly afraid.

They found Linda outside the front door and quickly brought her into the house. She had obviously been drinking, and heavily. Her arms held a full paper bag.

"Put this in your refrigerator," she said.

"I will. Thank you. We're glad you came," Grace said, giving her a quick hug. "Sit down here while I open up the bed in the guest room."

Linda dropped into the chair.

Silence drew an invisible curtain between the man and the woman. Neither moved to penetrate it; it stayed there until Grace returned.

"Now the room is ready. Would you like anything first, before you go to bed—a glass of milk, some coffee, or anything? No? Well, just follow me upstairs."

When Linda was settled, they went to the kitchen and opened the bag. It was filled with plastic bags of blood plasma, and administration sets of needles and tubing.

Neither spoke. When Grace had put the contents of the bag in the refrigerator, they stood with their arms around each other.

"Price must have left it for us," Grace said. "Dear Price— thinking of us, of Stephen, even when he was about to be tried and sent to the prison camp." She began to cry softly.

"You know," she continued after a few moments, "it makes me think of David, before he became king. You remember how he was holed up in the desert, and his men risked their lives to get a pitcher of water for him from behind the enemy lines— from his family well in Bethlehem. He poured the water out as an offering to the Lord."

"Well, we certainly won't do that—the time may come when Stephen needs it," Jon said hurriedly.

"I wasn't thinking of pouring this out. But I was thinking that Price didn't get back safely, like David's men did. I feel like praying. Dear God, thank you for Price and Linda. Thank you for Price's love for us. We know that to some extent—maybe to a great extent—we're the reason he's in Alaska. Do be near him, we pray. Show your love to him there, and to Linda here. Heal her, we ask. For Jesus' sake, Amen."

When they were back in bed, Jon said, "I guess Linda found that the light was going out in the tunnel."

"What do you mean?"

"She told me that drinking lit up the tunnel—her worry about Price and their little boy; that for a while it made life bearable. But I guess there was no light tonight."

"Poor Linda," Grace said, "I'm not sure I wouldn't find refuge in drink, too, if I didn't have another light in the tunnel. Especially if it were you who was in Alaska."

"I said something like that when she told me that about the tunnel. But you know, I don't find much light in our tunnel at present. These days God doesn't seem especially close to me at least. Sometimes I'm almost bitter about what he's done to Price and Linda, and what he's doing to your parents, and to Stephen."

"He's not doing it. The state is," Grace objected.

"But he put our rulers over us, didn't he? So he's responsible for extermination of old people, and the organ factory. And he's responsible for Stephen's hemophilia. He could have let him be born normal."

"I prayed that he would," Grace said.

"So did I."

"So God must have had some purpose in having him born the way he is."

"But what kind of purpose?" Jon asked. "He must know that hemophilia's a death warrant in America today."

"Dear, you have to go to work in a few hours. And I'll have to cope with Linda. So let's get some sleep now. Besides, we can't settle a heavy theological question at three in the morning."

While Jon was asleep he dreamed that Stephen was dead, and they couldn't find his body to bury. Then in a rapid shift, Jon and Grace were alone in a pine forest, scrabbling in the needles on the ground, digging a hole with their hands. In the hole they found a baby, a tiny boy baby, but it wasn't Stephen. And it was dead, freshly stillborn. They looked up to find Stephen hanging from the top of a tree. "See—I'm a Christmas tree ornament," he said. Then he disappeared again.

That was when Grace got up and brought back a light blanket, throwing it over them. He half awoke; the dream ended.

"You were talking, more like muttering in your sleep," Grace said. "You were probably cold."

"I was? I must have been dreaming."

"Why don't you turn on the wallscreen," Grace suggested. "It would probably help us get back to sleep."

"Okay," Jon answered. "But which one—the forest, or the country road, or the starry skies, or—"

"The one where waves are lapping up on the shore. It makes me think of Cape May." Then as Jon pressed buttons on the bed's headboard, "Yes, that's the one. It's really peaceful. But turn down the sound or we'll never get to sleep. I think you've accessed the wrong sound—that's more like a storm. There, that's better."

The wall opposite their bed was alight with an ocean stretching out to the horizon, and small waves coming in on a summer beach. The soft sound of their breaking filled the room. The slightly curved wall seemed to surround them with beach and ocean; it was as if they were lying out in the sun on a warm, carefree day. Soon they slept.

When they got up the next morning, Linda had left. The sofa bed in the guest room had been folded back together, and there was no indication that the room had been occupied for the past few hours, except a brief note, "Thanks. Linda."

"Poor Linda. I guess she didn't want to face us."

"Or she was afraid we really wouldn't understand, and be judgmental."

"I'll call her later today and thank her for the plasma," Grace said. "What a beautiful gift, from Price and her."

But when she did, she could get no answer, although she tried repeatedly.

Stephen was now back in school, walking and running without any sign of the previous trouble.

71

When a week went by without any indication that the authorities were aware of Price Berkowitz's treatment of Stephen, Jon and Grace were relieved. Their secret evidently was still safe. And they had the security of a supply of plasma.

If Jon and Grace were increasingly relieved as the days passed, George and Jean Duncan were increasingly burdened.

George no longer spoke of the number of days remaining. "It's fruitless," he said, "counterproductive."

"I agree, dear," Jean said. "Who knows how many days any of us has left? We'll just make each one a good day, like we've always tried in the past. God will help us."

George, however, didn't feel it was hopeless; he decided something must be done to help Price Berkowitz. With a sense of personal responsibility for the state's act of injustice toward the doctor, he wrote two letters. The first was to the Human Rights Commission of the United Nations. He did not go into detail, except to say that he thought the rights of a Jewish medical doctor named Price Berkowitz had been violated by the United States government.

Next he wrote to Soviet Premier Zamyatin, appealing for his intervention in the case of Doctor Price Berkowitz. "His only crime was helping people who were not helped by their own physicians. One example was my own grandson, who was born a hemophiliac, the same as the Czar's son before your revolution. You may know that such a birth is illegal here in the United States, and the baby is either aborted, or if he's born, sent to the organ factory. Now, six years later, they would still send that great little boy there. So Doctor Berkowitz helped us by getting some plasma, and transfusing it into him. Is this a criminal act, to prevent a boy just starting out in life from becoming a cripple? I am an ordinary man, an unimportant man, but I appeal to you to set the wheels of justice in motion for this Jewish doctor here in the United States."

He was careful not to give his name and address, although he considered first-class mail safe from tampering. It was good to live in the United States, in spite of everything.

When he mailed the letters, George was deeply satisfied. "I've done what I could," he told Jean.

"What do you mean?"

"I've written to the United Nations and to Premier Zamyatin of Russia. I've asked them to do something about that young Doctor Berkowitz. He hasn't had a square deal, being sent away to a prison camp in Alaska without a fair trial. Only bureaucrats who don't give a darn for human beings would convict him on evidence that only shows he helped people. So if people can try to get the UN to act when there's injustice in China or Poland, I guess I can try to get it to act when there's the same sort of injustice here in the United States. As we used to say, 'What's sauce for the goose is sauce for the gander.' We took the side of Sakharov and some of the others who were persecuted there in the past; why shouldn't they take the side of Berkowitz, when he's persecuted here now?"

Jean felt a vague sense of unease at her husband's action in writing the letters, but at that moment—before she could say anything—the conversation was interrupted by "It's Mrs. Leipert, your neighbor," spoken by someone at the open front door.

Jean brought her into the room, and she immediately said, "I hear that you got your termination notice, Mr. Duncan. Here—I brought you some flowers. They're from my garden. They may be the last ones before winter, so I wanted you to have them. Little enough you can do for a person, including your neighbor, in this life."

George thanked her and Jean found a vase.

"Yes," Jean said as she arranged the flowers—asters, chrysanthemums, black-eyed Susans and two roses—"George did get his seventy-fifth birthday present from the government."

"When's it for? How long do you have?"

"Until December twenty-second," George replied. "Then I say my good-bys and go to the thanotel."

"See, just like my Hughie. They gave him three months, too. You're the lucky ones, you know; sometimes there's one of the bureaucratic mixups and the person only gets two weeks. I tell you, that's when the pressure's on. Not that three months doesn't put pressure on you, too. I guess it's like the old days, when you could either have a coronary or linger on with cancer. Me, I'd have taken the coronary. My mother lingered for eleven months, and that was no picnic. She lived with us and I had all the nursing to do. Hughie said then, 'When I go, I hope it's a sudden thing, like a car accident or a heart attack. One moment you're something, big as life, the next moment you're nothing. Pffft!' My Hughie was a big man, big in all directions. He was also some years older than me. I've still got considerable years before I need to worry about my notice. And you, Mrs. Duncan, I judge you're enough younger than your mister that you don't have to worry, either. One of the side benefits of marrying young."

"I have six years," Jean said. "But to be honest, I wish I were George's age so we could go together."

"Don't say that! You may think that now, but you won't in another year. Excuse me for saying it, Mr. Duncan, but your wife needs hope, she needs to realize that, for her, all is not lost when you go to the thanotel. You have a daughter, don't you? And a grandchild—is it a grandson? There, what a lot you have to live for. And your beautiful home here. I've always admired how you kept the place up. It's lovely on the inside, too. I love this couch. They have beautiful rooms at the thanotel, you know. I heard all about it. Soft lights and gorgeous furniture. They must have paid a mint. And did you know, you can order anything in the wide world for your last meal? To eat and drink also. Best vintage wines, along with a stocked bar in every room. Some people even go in early in the day, before they have to, just to make the most of it."

"Your flowers are lovely," Jean interrupted. "Do they take a lot of your time?"

"Sure. Everything takes time."

"And time is what I'm running out of," George said. "Less than three months."

"Don't let it get you down. You've had seventy-five good

years. And it isn't too bad to go to sleep, never to wake up."

"Never to wake up? But I'm going to. You know life doesn't end with death."

"It doesn't? You don't mean to tell me that you think Hughie is still alive . . . someplace?"

"Certainly I do. The thanotel is just sort of a pause between here and there."

"I'm sure that believing something like that helps you face these next three months. My Hughie didn't believe in the hereafter, and neither do I. 'Leave the campsite a little better than you found it,' Hughie would say. 'For the next fellow, not for yourself. You'll never come back this way again.' Or any other way, for that matter. I hope you enjoy the flowers—they're past their peak, but still pretty. I must go now—I've wasted enough of your morning. And besides, Gimbels is having its fall clearance sale today, and I want to get there. Let me know if there's anything I can do," turning to Jean. "Don't get up, I'll find my way to the door."

"Well," Jean said, after Mrs. Leipert closed the door, "there goes Job's comforter."

Unexpectedly, George laughed, his first real laugh in several weeks, since he had received the notification to report to the thanotel. He laughed until tears ran down his cheeks.

Jean laughed, too. "But I really don't know what's so funny. She's really an awful woman, to come in here and say things like that."

"No, she's not. She was doing what she could, not just the flowers, but the way she talked. She felt she had to say something, to make conversation, and so she did. Only it got out of control. I'm not laughing at Mrs. Leipert."

"What are you laughing at, then?"

"At the fact that I've got it made. That I know the thanotel, or my ashes even, isn't the end of the line, just a transfer point."

"We should have told her why we believe that."

"There'll be another time, if I know Mrs. Leipert."

"And more comfort. Maybe next time she'll tell us whether she or Hughie drove their car to the thanotel."

George had stopped laughing. "Don't think I'll be going to the thanotel if I can help it. Not that I'm afraid to die, I'm not. But you still need me."

"Stephen and Grace do, too."

"I'll be interested to see what happens as a result of my letters. Now I'll just sit back and see if there's any justice left in the world. I hope I'll see it before—"

"If you don't see that one act of justice by then," Jean answered, "you'll not miss it. You'll never see an unjust act again. Oh, I wish the two of us could go at the same time."

"I still haven't decided that I'll go then," he replied with more confidence than he felt. And under his breath, "I've decided I won't."

She decided not to mention her uneasy feelings about the letters. After all, they were already mailed. And God could intervene, if her fears weren't groundless, as they well might be.

CAMP MEADE was a maximum security prison facility in the wilderness, fifty miles south of Barrow, Alaska. Fermi Mine, the great new uranium field, was nearby; it was there the prisoners worked.

The camp held seven thousand men and women, most of them political prisoners. Mixed in, however, were ordinary criminals. A third of the prison population was black; facilities and work crews were segregated.

Maximum security at Camp Meade was provided by nature rather than by barbed wire, manned towers and automatic guns. The camp's isolation and arctic climate during most of the year, impassable swamp during the few summer months, prevented escape. Mammoth buses transported the workers to the mine; otherwise no one ventured outside the buildings, which were connected by passageways, during most of the year.

Price Berkowitz was flown to Meade the night of his conviction, and after two weeks of orientation which included labor in the mines, was assigned to work in the prison hospital.

His sentence was indeterminate; by discreet questioning he learned that six years was probably the average term served by a first offender.

"But don't bank on it," his informant—a nurse—told him, "especially if you're here for political reasons. You won't get out until they think you're safe, or harmless, even if it means fifteen years."

The prison hospital's chief was a doctor assigned by the Army, a middle-aged woman. She was a colonel, always in uniform, and insisted on being addressed by everyone as Colonel Todd.

"Let's get one thing straight right at the outset," she said to Price. "You're a prisoner with paramedical skills here in the hospital. You're no longer a doctor. My judgment determines your actions.

"I see that you have most recently been on the surgical staff of Federal Hospital in Philadelphia. This means that you're good; it also means that you have much to unlearn. The medicine you practice here will be vintage nineteen-forty. We have no intensive care unit, no patient monitoring devices, no computerized diagnostic procedures. The federal government doesn't believe in pampering the kind of prisoners we have here at Meade.

"You will set broken arms and legs, mend skulls, remove tumors and organs—but no transplants. Your job will be to get prisoners back to work as quickly as possible, or else buried. Actually, cremated. Do you understand?"

"Yes, Colonel Todd."

"Good. Now one other thing: I see that you violated the law and professional standards by caring for other doctors' patients. We will not tolerate such conduct here. You can, by a stroke of my pen, be transferred to work in the mines. The life expectancy there, incidentally, is not so good as that of a paramedic here in the hospital. You will be expected to report to the hospital tomorrow morning and every morning thereafter at six-thirty. You may go now."

The prisoners slept in huge barracks, men and women together. Price had found an empty bunk, on the third tier above the floor. As he prepared for bed that night, he noticed a man several bunks away reading a worn black Bible.

"Alyoshka," Price called. "Imagine finding you here."

The man looked around at Price. "What? I don't understand. My name's Majdowski."

"Never mind. Sometime I may want to borrow that Bible."

"Good. But who did you think I was?"

"A Russian friend of mine. I first met him in high school. Good night. He was a really great guy."

As day followed day, Price found that in many respects Camp Meade was as bad as its Soviet counterparts, about which he had read; in others it was better. The food was much better, not a high-protein diet, but not watery cabbage soup, either. Caloric intake seemed to be sufficient to maintain health, even for those who worked at hard manual labor. He saw no instances of malnutrition.

Waste disposal, on the other hand, was right out of *Ivan Denisovitch,* and probably for the same reasons. Permafrost made a septic system impossible. So slop pails were picked up and emptied every morning.

"Good food and flush toilets—hell, they're nonessentials," Price said one night to the Bible-reading prisoner, whom he had come to respect and trust through many conversations together. "The essential is human dignity, respect for the human condition—and that's as lacking here as it ever was in Russia."

"You know," the prisoner replied, putting down his Bible, "first time they make me take my shit and wipe it all over my face, I think I never have dignity again. But then I realize that dignity is in that direction—" pointing up past the rafters—"not in this—" pointing around the barracks, "or even this—" touching his finger to his chest.

"On line, Alyoshka. Best sermon I ever heard."

The man picked up his Bible again, then pointed it at Price: "You have this dignity, too, by taking Jesus into your heart."

"Damn it," Price said, "now you've spoiled the sermon."

For many men and women, Price reflected, life is a round of commitments to friends and possessions, with frequent necessary decisions each day. His own medical decisions had often been life-or-death ones. He recalled how he had welcomed a break of pace, the divestiture of responsibility, simple schedules planned by others. This was the reason he had found so much enjoyment in camping with Linda and their friends, whether backpacking or canoeing.

Now, to his surprise, he was finding that prison-camp life, like those rugged excursions, was a not unwelcome change from his experience in recent years. Its regularity, its schedule—even though the days were long—its freedom from the necessity of decision-making, all contributed to an initial feeling of well-being.

Only his concern for Linda and his son, he realized, a concern that deepened each day, kept him from settling in, completely settling in. They were constantly at the front of his mind. Was Linda coping, or was she living out an alcoholic nightmare? Where was young Price—with Linda, or with his grandmother? He forced himself not to think of another possibility, the Center for Life Support Systems.

He often thought of Grace and Jon, and Stephen, with warm affection. He knew that they had not been involved in the case brought against him by the government; even if they had, it probably would not have changed his feelings toward them.

Faced with a mounting fear for his wife and son, one night he brought up the matter of prayer to the prisoner with a Bible.

"Alyoshka, can God take care of people who are in danger?"

"Of course he can. —Why can't you remember my name? I told you, it's not Alyoshka. —But look at David, in the Bible. King Saul was out to kill him—"

"How can you get God to take care of someone you're afraid for?"

"Pray. That's all there is to it."

79

"But how do you pray? What do you say?"

"Look, you talk to me, don't you? Talk to God. Tell him what's on your mind."

"That's all there is to it?"

"Sure. Except you pray in Jesus' name."

"What does that have to do with it? And how can I pray that way when I'm a Jew—I don't believe in Jesus. I'm surprised to find I may even believe in God."

"You stupid? Jesus himself was a Jew."

"But we lost him."

"So was Peter. And Matthew. Saint Paul—all of them was Jews."

"All right, you've made your point."

"You want dignity in this filthy hole: you ask Jesus for it. You want prayers answered: you ask Jesus for it."

"You made it twice."

Before he went to sleep that night, Price spoke into the rolled-up pants he used for a pillow: "God, here I am wanting to talk to you. You know me, I guess, even though I don't know you. You know Linda, my wife, too, and Price, my unfortunate little son. I want to ask you to take care of them tonight and tomorrow, and all the time I'm away from them. I didn't do such a good job taking care of Linda while I was there, sir—you must know her alcohol problem, and that to a considerable extent I'm responsible for it. I'm sorry. Somehow, tonight, let her know I love her. I don't know how to end this, so good night."

He had a good feeling as he went to sleep moments later; he wasn't quite so worried.

Two weeks passed. One day, a Thursday, Colonel Todd called Price into her office. A subtle change in her attitude surprised him.

"Doctor Berkowitz"—he didn't understand her use of the title; the colonel had previously only addressed him by his last name—"I have just received your records from the Pentagon. I find that you were an unusually skilled surgeon in the transplant unit at Federal Hospital in Philadelphia. It is about this that I want to talk to you. What is the status of kidney transplants at the present time?"

80

"Eighty percent effective, even higher with children."

"And no special equipment is necessary, such as would be the case with heart or liver transplant?"

"No. Just the dialysis machine. I might add that with patients under twenty-five years of age, we're now transplanting two kidneys, from separate donors. This almost guarantees a trouble-free future."

"Good. Now for the reason I've asked these questions. The commanding general of the Alaska command, located in Fairbanks, has a fourteen-year-old son with no renal function. For the past three months he's been on dialysis.

"The general has received repeated medical advice to take his son to Walter Reed, or another transplant center such as Federal in Seattle, and have a kidney transplant. However, his wife is herself a problem, in need of psychiatric attention. Actually, she refuses to have the boy taken down to the lower forty-eight. She thinks he'll die there. The general stands by her in this, and asks why the army medical service can't take care of his son in the Fairbanks hospital."

"You could quite easily, with the right surgical procedure and skill in immunosuppressives."

"Exactly. And so I am . . . asking you to perform this transplant operation, actually two operations, if I understood you correctly."

"Only one. We do both kidneys at the same time."

"Good. I will inform the general and secure the donors. What are the optimum requirements as to age and sex?"

"Under age thirty, one male, one female. We think there's a slight edge to a female who has recently aborted. But of course, it's virtually impossible to meet those optimum requirements. So do the best you can, or the best that comes along in the way of brain-dead cadavers."

"We can secure the optimum with living donors."

An alarm bell rang in Price's brain. "Hey, no forced donors. Nobody uses living ones anymore, not with the fully effective new immunosuppressives. There is still such a thing as the Hippocratic oath, even in a prison camp."

"All right. No living donors. How long will a kidney keep after removal?"

"Five to seven days under stringent storage requirements. But it's better to transplant immediately."

"Be prepared to fly to Fairbanks and perform the surgery at any time, Doctor Berkowitz."

Several days later, Price received a message to go at once to Colonel Todd's office. She rose from her desk and greeted him with a handshake.

"Lady luck has smiled on us. A young couple were riding a motorcycle in Fairbanks and had an accident with a semi-trailer. Neither was wearing a helmet; they are both clinically dead, with flat EEG readings and no oxygen to the brain. Bodily functions are being maintained by life-support systems. So we will take a flight to Fairbanks immediately. Your clothes, the ones you wore when you came here, are in the outside office. Be quick, Doctor Berkowitz. I will go to Fairbanks with you."

Price changed his clothes and was driven to the airport with Colonel Todd. They did not talk much on the plane. The sky was cloudless; Price enjoyed his view of the barren Alaskan wilderness.

At the hospital, Price examined the operating room, the intensive care unit and monitoring provisions, and was satisfied.

"We might as well get on with it. You have all the drugs I ordered for the postsurgical care?"

"Yes. They were flown in this morning."

Price was deeply affected, as he had always been, by the sight of the terribly damaged young man and woman, both black, scarcely into their twenties. Their heads were badly crushed; even without looking at the EEG, he knew they could never have survived the accident. Other bones were broken, but their kidneys were intact.

When the artificial breathing machines were removed, another doctor certified their deaths, and Price immediately removed both kidneys from each. One set could be stored for another recipient; it would probably be flown to Walter Reed.

Other physicians had already prepared the general's son for

surgery. Price, after changing gowns and going through a fresh scrub, removed the boy's diseased kidneys and implanted the new ones. Later those who assisted him in the operation complimented him on his skill.

"Now the tough part begins," he said after the transplant. "This next week will require twenty-four hours of extreme watchfulness every day, to see that the drugs function properly and the kidneys are accepted."

The monitoring began. Price only slept an hour or two at a time during the week. He sat for long hours in front of the computer video-readout terminal, implementing an ever-changing drug regimen.

Finally, at week's end, he turned from the screen to Colonel Todd and said, "They've taken. Both kidneys have been accepted. In two or three days the boy can be taken out of isolation and intensive care, and in a month he can begin to play baseball again."

During the week, Price tried numerous times to reach Linda by a collect phone call, but was unsuccessful each time. He did not call the Stantons or anyone else out of regard for their safety.

Price met the general, who expressed his appreciation in formal language, and the general's wife, who tearfully kissed him, before he was flown back to Camp Meade. Colonel Todd stayed behind, "to see the sights of Fairbanks" for a few days. She invited Price to stay with her, but he turned the invitation down.

By the ever-surprising prison grapevine, everyone seemed to know all about Price's mission in Fairbanks, and its success. He noticed, however, not without disappointment, a new attitude of reserve toward him, instead of the former openness.

That night he was glad for a renewed opportunity to talk to his Bible-reading friend in the barracks.

"Alyoshka, it's good to see you again."

"And good to see you, sir, back again, safe and sound."

"Tell me, why is everyone so distant toward me, including you?"

"You must know, sir."

"Why—because I've cooperated with the establishment, so now I'm tainted? Do people really think I'll be a—what's it called—a stoolie, from here on in? Surely you don't think that— you know I just did what any doctor would do, helping a boy live?"

"No sir, I don't think that. And I don't think many others do, either. It's . . . Caesar and Vonette."

"Caesar and Vonette? What are you talking about?"

"Don't you know?"

"Of course not. Hurry up and tell me." As he spoke, an awful suspicion began to possess his mind.

"They're a young couple loves each other in barracks nine. That's a black barracks. You know, a girl can't have a baby in prison camp; she was aborted several weeks before you get here. Just before you fly down to Fairbanks, they're flown there with three worst guards. Guards return without them."

Price slid off his bunk and vomited into the slop pail.

PRICE DIDN'T sleep. He went over the incident again and again, and his involvement in it. He was not guilty of any moral or professional transgression, but he felt guilty. He felt unclean.

How should he react now that the facts, for he had no doubt they were true, were in his possession? Could he continue to practice medicine—for it was that, even though he was not accorded the status of a doctor—under Colonel Todd?

What about those medical doctors and researchers who had worked in Hitler's concentration camps? Were any of them innocent, really innocent, of involvement in atrocities against the Jews? Against his own grandfather and grandmother?

He saw the battered skulls and bodies of the young black man and woman. He felt their kidneys in his hands. He, Price Berkowitz, Jewish M.D., had done that.

But if he spoke out in protest, he'd be removed from the hospital staff and be put to work in the mines. The significant factor here wasn't the hard labor—he felt up to that. It would probably be good for him. But it could delay or jeopardize his return to Linda and young Price.

Another thing. If he continued in the hospital, especially now that he had demonstrated professional skill and been the means of renewed health for the Alaska Command general's son, he would be in a strong position to help other prisoners, to bring influence to bear against the evil system.

On the other hand, his fellow prisoners would perceive him as a part of that evil, a member of the conspiracy. They would probably reject his help, distrust it.

Moses. There was a man. Perhaps it was Alyoshka's loud snoring that made him think of a precedent in the Torah. But did his fellow Jews trust Moses after he killed a man—one of the oppressors, at that—and intervened in their own behalf? No, they rejected his help, said they feared he would kill them, too.

Back and forth he went in his tug-of-war, first pulling on one side of the line, then running across it to pull on the other. One way or another, he repeated the arguments again and again. He could not decide what to do.

After several hours, he gave up. Perhaps this was one of those problems that he wouldn't have to decide, that would be decided for him by others.

At any rate, he would make no move until Colonel Todd returned.

The next day, he found a new attitude of respect, even deference, toward him in the hospital. Army personnel, not prisoners, addressed him as Doctor Berkowitz. There were several requests for his consultation and help. He liked the change in the hospital climate; at the same time he knew that to like it too much would tip the scales in the decision he faced.

At the beginning of the following week, Colonel Todd was back in her office. She summoned Price, rising and coming around to the front of her desk when he appeared at the door.

"And how is my skillful colleague?" She put an arm around his shoulders. "Our patient is recovering nicely, and his parents—especially the general—asked me to convey their deep appreciation."

"Thank you," he said. "My surgical residency was thanks to the Army, so I suppose— Now I should like to ask you for a favor."

"Of course I shall do it, if it's in my power. What is it?"

"I'd like to request a transfer from my duty here in the hospital to the mines, or some other work assignment."

She was silent for a moment. "Why?"

"Caesar and Vonette. And the whole damned system."

"Caesar and Vonette?" She stared blankly at him. "I don't get it."

"The black kids who 'donated' their kidneys to the general's son."

Her eyes narrowed, her face became even harder.

"Now let's just cut this short," Price said, "and you pass along my request for a change in assignment. My reasons don't need to go any further than this office. If they do, I'll be glad to speak in support of my ethical position."

"Ethical position—hell. What do you think brought you here, to Meade, in the first place?"

"Please just pass my request along. If it takes a few days, I'll be willing to continue here at the hospital until the transfer comes through." He was trying hard to control himself.

"Damn you. Do you realize that you've passed judgment on all the rest of us?"

He was silent.

She went back to her desk and sat down.

"Do you realize that most of the Negroes in this camp are communist revolutionaries, that they're here because they've

86

plotted to overthrow the United States government? Especially the younger ones, those under thirty."

He didn't speak.

"If this were wartime, those black sons-of-machs would be executed, shot for treason. But since it's not, the government sends them here." She paused for a moment, then continued, "You're willing to throw over your future, throw away years— maybe your practice of medicine itself, for those black communist bastards?"

Price answered calmly, "For human beings, like you and me."

"Human beings? Those niggers weren't worth your little toe. You'd throw your whole life away for them? Don't make me laugh. Let's just forget this conversation and you get back to work . . Berkowitz." She picked up some papers and began shuffling them.

He stood and waited.

Finally she looked up and shouted, "I told you to get back to work."

"You haven't said you'll pass my request for a transfer along."

"I won't. So get back to your job."

"In that case I shall ask to see the prison commander, and pass on to him my knowledge of what occurred."

"Do you think he doesn't know? Who do you think has to approve the forms that are sent to Washington for prisoners who die or disappear? And who do you think approves my recommendation that a patient who is . . . disturbed . . . gets sent to the mental unit? Or decides that he'd do better in isolation? I'll give you one minute to go through that door and get back to work."

"You know something," he said, "you can't maintain such a system forever. Hitler was going great guns for a long time, Jews were being put to death in gas ovens, doctors were experimenting on their victims. Then it stopped. Like that. Remember the Nuremberg trials?"

"Damn it. You can't threaten an officer of the United States Army." She was silent for several moments, looking past Price into space. Then she pressed a button and an aide appeared. "Put in a call for the guards, and have them take this man to the commander's office. Fill in the necessary forms for transfer to another work assignment. Bring them back and I'll sign them. At once."

"What reason shall I give, Colonel Todd?" the aide asked.

"Unsatisfactory performance of duties."

She didn't look up as Price left the office.

GEORGE DUNCAN'S letter to the United Nations Commission on Human Rights produced quick action. He had a visit from a tall young man with a British accent, who identified himself as a staff lawyer.

The Commission representative wanted to ascertain that he was, in fact, the George Duncan who had written protesting against the United States violation of the rights of Price Berkowitz—rights protected by the Commission's charter.

George was cautious. Before he answered, he asked to see the visitor's credentials.

The man produced a British passport, with his photograph, and a notarized letter authorizing him to represent the Commission on Human Rights in an investigation of the complaint lodged for Price Berkowitz, M.D. He would guarantee confidentiality to any statement George might make, or answers he might give.

How, George asked, had the man located him, since he had not included his address in the letter?

A simple matter. The letter was postmarked and there were only two other George M. Duncans in the greater Philadelphia area. He had visited the others, and was convinced they had not written the letter.

With a repeated guarantee of secrecy from his visitor, George admitted that he had indeed written the letter.

The representative then asked whether he had any reason to suspect that the government's action was racially or religiously inspired—that is, was it related to anti-Semitism?"

"No," George replied, "Doctor Berkowitz is a Jew, but I wasn't protesting that angle. I think they'd have been as likely to punish a Christian in the same way—that is, someone who wasn't a Jew. What I wrote to complain about was that he was being punished for helping people, something a doctor ought to do. But this senseless bureaucracy just felt he ought to be limited to helping people they assigned to him."

In that case, the representative told him, the case did not lie within the jurisdiction of the Human Rights Commission. He should seek redress for Doctor Berkowitz through the United States courts, perhaps lodging a habeas corpus action. With that, the British lawyer left.

George had another visitor the same day.

The FBI agent didn't phone, but appeared at the Duncans' door that afternoon. He asked George to answer some questions. At first George was not apprehensive; evidently there had been a leak in the UN Commission—perhaps the United States representative. But he had foreseen this possibility when he wrote the letter, and had only lodged a general complaint. Nothing could connect Doctor Berkowitz with Stephen.

"First, I must warn you," the agent said after he was seated across from George in the living room, "that you may refuse to answer my questions, or may request that counsel be present. While you will not be testifying under oath, there are penalties for lying to an agent of the Federal Bureau of Investigation. In addition, anything you say may be used against you. Do you fully understand what I have told you?"

"Yes," George said, "I have nothing to hide. Just go on."

The agent began to write in a notebook.

"First, what is your full name?"

"George MacLeod Duncan."

"How old are you?"

"Just turned seventy-five."

"Are you married?"

"Yes, Jean's upstairs, having a nap."

"What is your wife's full name, including her family name?"

"Jean Ross Duncan."

"How old is she?"

"Sixty-nine. Say, are all these questions really necessary?"

"They are. How long have you lived at this address?"

"Eight years."

"Do you have any sons or daughters?"

"Yes. A daughter."

"Is she married? And is she your only child?"

"Yes to both of those questions."

"What are her and her husband's names?"

"Grace and Jon Stanton."

"Did you, about ten days ago, write a letter to the Human Rights Commission of the United Nations, protesting United States treatment of Price Berkowitz, M.D., formerly employed by Federal Hospital, Philadelphia?"

"I did."

"Do Jon and Grace Stanton have any children? And their names, please."

"Yes, they have a son, Stephen."

"What is their home address?"

"Uh, 517 Auden Avenue, Wayne, Pennsylvania."

"What was your relation to Price Berkowitz?"

"Rather casual. I met him at the home of—" suddenly George was staring into a pit, the possible consequences of his action on behalf of Price—"mutual friends. Would you like some coffee?"

"No thanks. Who were these friends?"

"I don't believe I'm at liberty to tell you that."

"Did you write a letter, or letters, to any other representative of a foreign government, or political entity, in addition to the

90

United Nations Commission on Human Rights, about Price Berkowitz, M.D.?"

George was silent for a long moment. "I don't believe I'll answer that question."

"I shall note here that you refused to answer the two questions. And I suppose the reason is your right to avoid self-incrimination?"

"My reason is that it's none of your darn business. Up until today I have had a pretty high opinion of the FBI. Now you have raised some questions in my mind."

"I regret that. Now, will you read through my notes and sign that this is a true statement of your replies to my questions asked in the interview. If you cannot read my handwriting, I shall read the notes aloud to you."

"I can read it." And after several minutes of careful reading, "However, I won't sign it."

"Here, I'll attach this printed statement at the bottom. If you sign this, it will save you from more interviews."

"I'm sorry, I refuse to sign it," George said, and passed the sheets of paper back to the agent.

"Well, thanks for your cooperation in the interview anyway. Good-by."

For a long time after the agent left, George sat staring into space, thinking.

By his intervention on behalf of Price Berkowitz, with the best of intentions, had he brought danger into the lives of Grace and Jon . . . and Stephen? He had not foreseen the possibility that the government would learn about his letter, nor that the question would be asked about how he knew Price. He had almost answered the question and told the agent about Jon and Grace's acquaintance with Dr. Berkowitz.

And that question about whether he had written to any other government. Did they know about his letter to Premier Zamyatin, his attempt to enlist the Russian government's help? He had felt so secure in his belief that the government didn't tamper with first class mail. But evidently they did, or at least with a letter addressed to the top Soviet official. He hadn't signed the letter or included a return address, but he had mailed it from a box near his home. And he hadn't worn gloves when he handled it, or wiped it off before sealing it—that would have seemed unnecessary, melodramatic even. Now he realized that they probably had some fingerprints, if not other evidence more sophisticated than he could even imagine, to link the letter to him, George Duncan. He was aghast at his stupidity, at his terrible blunder.

He had mentioned his hemophilic grandson in that letter. He had told how Price helped him. Helped Stephen. He, Stephen's grandfather, God forbid, may have betrayed his dear grandson to the government. His hands shook, his heart skipped beats as he considered the terrible possibility.

When Jean came downstairs from her nap, he told her about the FBI agent's visit, and his fear.

"We don't know that anything will come of it," she said. "Let's not worry dear Grace and Jon about it. Surely, when you only did what you did to help Doctor Berkowitz, we can trust God with the results."

"But all the results recently seem to be coming out bad."

"Not all. Stephen is back in school, remember?"

"I wish I could believe that nothing will come of it. But somehow—" His voice trailed off.

Jon and Grace stopped at their home a few nights later, with Stephen.

"We wondered how you were," Grace said. "It's been several days since we've seen you."

"We're fine," Jean assured her. "And how's your leg, Stephen?"

"Great, grandma. I can play most of the games at school with the other kids now."

"Wonderful," George Duncan said, pulling Stephen over to sit on his lap. "How would you like to take a trip with me?"

"Dad, whatever are you talking about?" Grace asked.

"Yes, George, what kind of an idea is that? You haven't said anything to me about any trip." Jean looked at him anxiously.

"Oh, just an idea I had. Probably won't amount to a hill of beans, but I was thinking that maybe Stephen and I should go away somewhere together. How about it?"

"I'd like to, grandpa. Where'll we go?"

"Maybe to Russia."

"Dad, will you stop joking? You know Stephen will take you seriously."

"Did you ever think I might be serious? After all, your friend Doctor Berkowitz suggested such a trip for Jean and me, and maybe we should take Stephen along. We'd find asylum there."

"That'd be great. Could mother and daddy come too?" Stephen asked.

"If they wanted to. That would be sort of like colonizing a new country."

"Like the Pilgrims did," Stephen said excitedly.

"Dad, this has gone far enough." Grace's tone revealed her exasperation.

"You wouldn't really emigrate to a communist country, would you, Mr. Duncan?" Jon's use of formal address was unusual; it showed his concern.

"Why not? Don't you want to see me live? And wouldn't you like to see your son safe?"

"He's safe here. But let's not talk about such things when he's around."

"I told you my leg was well, grandpa."

"Yes, Stephen—You say don't talk about it. Don't talk about it. Everything will be all right. But maybe everything won't be all right. Maybe in a few days everything will come crashing down around our heads. I think I'll just go to bed." He helped Stephen off his lap and stood up.

"George dear, don't leave us. Why, Grace and Jon have just come. We're not saying we'll never talk about it—just that right now doesn't seem appropriate. You know I'm—we're all as deeply concerned as you are."

George remained standing. "Are you? Are you really concerned that in two months I'll go into the thanotel to die?"

"Of course we are, dear dad." Grace came over and kissed

93

him. "It's on our minds every waking hour, that unless God intervenes, we're going to lose you . . . for a time."

"But you'll gain Christ, which St. Paul tells us is far better," Jon added.

"I'm not St. Paul. I'm George Duncan. St. Paul wasn't married, he didn't have a wife like Jean to leave behind. Nor a grandson like Stephen, my dear Stephen. So maybe, just maybe, he could say something that I can't say—and mean it. Good night." And he went down the hall to the bedroom, closing the door behind him.

"Poor dad," Grace said as she sat down again. "The strain is too much for him."

"Maybe poor us," Jean said quietly, "that we can't see things from his point of view."

"Which at this moment is hardly Christian," Jon said.

"I'm not so sure. I'm not so sure." Jean began to pace up and down the room as she spoke. Her voice quivered.

"You're not, mother?"

"No, I don't know how to put this, but it seems to me that God wants us to be honest with him and with each other, almost above anything else. George was being honest. He has deep questions about why God allows everything that's going on. It's not just his own appointment with death, at the thanotel, it's Doctor Berkowitz and his wife, it's—most of all, it's Stephen. I almost think he could take his own situation, hard though it is, if it weren't for the other."

"We know what you're saying, Jean," Jon said, "but can't we trust God, even in this?"

"I'm not sure George isn't trusting God. He'd just like some answers. And when I think about the Bible, I don't just think about St. Paul, and his contentment with persecution and his approaching death. Maybe George is right, that Paul might have had a little different outlook if he'd had a wife and a grandchild, if he'd settled down and not been traveling all the time. But whether that's so or not, I seem to remember that Jeremiah had some pretty hard questions for God, when he was facing death.

And there were others—Habakkuk, for instance—who didn't hesitate to speak out when they thought God wasn't being fair." She sat down wearily in the chair. "And even Jesus, on the cross, asked why."

"I saw Linda Berkowitz again," Grace said. "She stopped at the house this afternoon. And she hadn't been drinking."

"I'm so glad, dear. And what did you talk about—how's her little boy?"

"He's fine, that is, there's no problem with the government yet. And she has him back home with her—isn't that wonderful? Her next-door neighbor, a widow named Anna Shulker—a real down-to-earth woman, I've met her—was taking care of the little boy while Linda came to see me."

"I guess she hasn't heard anything from her husband."

"That's one thing she wanted to tell me. It seems she had a phone call from someone at Federal Hospital. She doesn't know who it was, but he said they'd had an urgent request for a certain kind of drugs to be sent to the hospital in Fairbanks, Alaska. When they asked for details, this person explained to Linda, they were told that a surgeon who had formerly been on their staff was going to do a kidney transplant on an army officer's son. The obvious person seemed to be Price. Linda was so excited—she's sure it really was Price."

"I'm glad she's had that encouragement. Any kind of hope is a help when you're just waiting."

"Yes, and do you know what else she said? That maybe there is a God who listens to us when we pray. That was it, maybe there really is a God who listens when we turn to him and pray."

"If she could just come to know him."

"Is there anything we can do for you, mother?" Jon stood up. "We can sense how difficult these days are for you."

Jean's eyes filled with tears. "No, dear Jon, except pray. There's more to it than George said tonight—he's worried about something, something that's not related to his own death. That's all I can say, but do pray for us—especially for George."

"We will—we do," Jon assured her. "And if I can help with

that other thing, mother, whatever it is, the thing that's on dad's mind, you'll let me know, won't you?"

"Yes, I will. You and Grace are such a help."

IT WAS ABOUT ten o'clock the next morning when the FBI agent arrived at the offices of Stern International, identified himself and asked to see Jonathan Stanton.

"Coggan, Fred Coggan, special agent of the Federal Bureau of Investigation," he introduced himself to Jon. "I wish to ask certain questions. You are free to refuse to answer, or to ask for the presence of counsel—your lawyer—when you are interviewed. But any answers you do give must be truthful; there are penalties for lying to an agent. Also, anything you say may be used in future legal proceedings against you. Is that clear?"

Jon said that it was. His heart was pounding—what would cause the FBI to want to question him at this point?

"All right then, I shall proceed." The agent produced a legal tablet and pen. "Your full name, please, and address."

"Jonathan Albright Stanton, 517 Auden Avenue, Wayne."

"Your wife's full name."

"Grace Duncan Stanton."

"Same address?"

"Yes."

"Do you have a child?"

"Yes."

"His name."

Why had he said "his" name? Jon wondered. His fear increased.

"Stephen George Stanton."

96

"His age?"

"Six."

"Were you acquainted with a surgeon, lately of this city, whose name was Price Berkowitz?"

"Yes, I was." Jon suddenly felt weak.

"How did you know him? Under what circumstances?"

"Socially. We—that is, my wife and I—were acquainted with Doctor Berkowitz and his wife."

"Did he ever come to your home?"

"Of course."

"For what purpose?"

"Oh, we talked and had coffee together."

"Did he come to your home to treat your son, that is, provide medical attention?"

"Doctor Berkowitz was not our doctor. We have our own physician, to whom we're assigned. He takes care of our health needs."

"You have not answered my question, Mr. Stanton. When Price Berkowitz came to your home, did he provide medical care for your son?"

Jon answered in a small voice, "Yes, he did." His answer could not hurt Price further, and somehow the FBI must have had the damning information already, or they wouldn't be asking the question.

"Was that treatment related to your son's hemophilia?"

Jon was prepared for the question, but it still hit him hard. He couldn't answer.

"Did Price Berkowitz treat your son's hemophilia?"

"Actually, it was a hip injury—bleeding into the socket. No diagnosis of hemophilia has ever been made."

"Where was your son Stephen born?"

"In this city. That is, in Wayne."

"There's no hospital in Wayne, is there?"

"He was born at home."

For the first time, the agent showed surprise. "I never heard of anyone being born at home these days."

Jon was silent.

"Who is your assigned physician?"

"Doctor R. G. Anderson."

"Is he aware of your son's hemophilia?"

"No, he goes strictly by the book. So we've never told him, and we were able to handle everything until the hip injury." Jon paused as he realized the admission he had made. He continued in a low, hopeless, voice, "Then we asked Doctor Berkowitz—but like I said earlier, no diagnosis of hemophilia has ever been made. So obviously Doctor Anderson wouldn't know our son had a condition that we—his mother and I—don't even know he has."

"Thank you. I think I understand your answer. One more question: What is the name of the child's maternal grandfather?"

"George Duncan. But I don't see where he enters into this matter."

"Perhaps he doesn't. Now I'm going to read back all my questions and all your answers to you, and if you agree that the written report of the interview is correct, I'll ask you to sign a statement to that effect. Do you understand what I am saying?"

After the agent left, Jon sat at his desk, his head in his hands. He had a pounding headache.

Stephen. His dear son Stephen. His only son Stephen, the fruit of his love for Grace. Stephen betrayed, suddenly facing death—the living death of the organ factory. He wept silently.

His secretary came into the office, said "Oh—excuse me," and left. He was only faintly aware of the interruption. He turned on the readout terminal and called up the figures on new home starts. But he couldn't concentrate. He stood and walked over to the window.

Who had betrayed Stephen? Who had alerted the authorities to his condition? Certainly not Price or Linda—he doubted that Price would do so, even under physical torture. And Linda had her own little boy to consider. But who would betray them, betray Stephen?

"Philip Allen. Doctor Philip Allen." He said the name aloud.

Who knew about the hip injury, and the hemophilia, in the

first place? Who had talked to Price Berkowitz? He was suddenly sure that Philip Allen had not only betrayed Stephen, but Price Berkowitz as well. Doctor Philip Allen, wolf in sheep's clothing, mouthing spiritual truths in church while he was a Judas outside church.

"God, repay him," he prayed. "You say that vengeance is yours, not ours, so exercise it against Philip Allen. Think of Stephen, Price and Linda, and of Grace and me, and pay him back. Pay Doctor Philip Allen back." He started to say, "For Jesus' sake," but didn't finish it.

Should he tell Grace? He touched the phone, then moved his hand back from it. No, he'd wait until tonight—and maybe not even tell her then.

By the time he got home that night, he had decided to tell Grace everything. She would be better able to cope, if Coggan or some other FBI agent called at the house to question her.

"Do you really think it was Philip Allen?" Grace asked, after he had told her all about the interview and his subsequent suspicion.

"I'm sure of it. Nobody else had all the facts—or if they did, they'd die rather than hurt Stephen."

"I can't believe that a Christian brother would do that."

"He's no more a brother than Judas was. He's a betrayer, a wolf in sheep's clothing."

"Even so, if you're right—which I'm not sure of at this point—you'd better be sure that your response is Christian. Jesus said to love your enemies—"

"Love Doctor Philip Allen? Love a wolf in sheep's clothing, a Judas?"

"That's what Jesus said. And remember that he even called Judas 'friend,' when Judas came out to the garden and betrayed him."

Jon was silent.

"Besides, you could be wrong. About Philip Allen being the one, that is."

"I'm right, you'll find out I'm right. Anyway, we might as

well throw out the blood plasma that's in the refrigerator, and get some space for other things. We'll never need it."

Grace found it hard to speak. "Jon, we can't give up hope. God is able to save us—to save dear Stephen—even out of this awful situation."

"I hope so. Let's go to bed—I just feel like sleeping. In fact, I wish I could go to sleep and never wake up."

"Or wake up and find it's all just a dream—a nightmare."

They went to bed, but could not go to sleep, even after Jon turned the wallscreen on to a tropical forest with the sound of rain falling.

The next morning the mailman delivered a registered letter. Grace signed for it, then could hardly force herself to open it when she saw the sender's name: American Medical Association—United States Department of Health, Philadelphia.

The letter was formal, a court order to report to Federal Hospital the following Tuesday with Stephen George Stanton, their son. Penalties for disregarding the order were explained.

She phoned Jon at his office. As soon as he saw her face on the videoscreem, he said, "What's wrong?"

"We've received the notice about Stephen. We have to take him to Federal Hospital next week. It's a court order."

Jon was silent. He had nothing to say.

"I'm sorry to bother you like this at the office," Grace went on, "but I thought you'd want to know right away."

"I do. Where's Stephen?"

"At school, of course. What can we do?"

"I don't know. It seems like a dead end, a real one this time. But let's not say any more on the phone. We can talk about it later tonight."

"All right, dear. By the way, you do remember that you promised to take Stephen somewhere after supper, don't you? He's looking forward to it."

"Of course I remember. I think we'll go to the electronic maze in the park. Maybe you'll want to come along," Jon suggested.

"Maybe I will. Each moment is precious, isn't it?"

"Don't give up. Something may happen."

"Something has to happen." The videoscreen was suddenly blank. But Grace continued to look at it for a long time.

ON FRIDAY morning, just after Jon left, Grace phoned Ruth Swanson.

Ruth's face on the videophone was radiant as she recognized Grace. "I've been wondering when you'd call," she said.

"Do you remember that you offered to have Stephen anointed for healing?" Grace asked, her tone as well as her facial expression indicating her anxiety.

"Do you think I'd forget? And now you want me to make the arrangements. Is that right? Praise the Lord!"

Grace's face brightened. "You will? How long will it take?"

"We could do it tonight. But how about Sunday? We have a time for anointing after the evening service."

"Wonderful. We'll be there." Grace could feel a weight drop away from her heart.

"Now you realize that you and Jon have to have faith, if your little boy is to be healed—and to stay healed. James says in his Epistle that you can't waver. If you do, it's like the waves of the sea. So I think I should tell you this ahead of time. We can anoint, but you must have faith for the healing to take place." Ruth said it with great seriousness.

"I know that, or at least I think I do. And I'll explain it to Jon. But how can you keep from sometimes wavering?" Grace looked worried again.

"Only believe," Ruth replied. "That's all there is to it: only believe. Jesus said that if you believe, you can say to this mountain, 'Be removed,' and it will be removed. But you can't doubt. Believe that it has happened and it will happen. It's as simple as that."

"Thank you," Grace said. "I'll try. So will Jon."

"Trying isn't enough. It's like wavering. You have to make up your mind to it, exclude every thought of failure. Once you allow the thought to enter, 'Maybe it won't happen,' you're lost. And so is your son."

"I'll remember that," Grace said. "I really will."

"Why don't we stop for you Sunday evening, about six-thirty? Then I won't have to give you directions over the phone."

"Would you?" Grace replied. "That would be so kind of you."

That night at dinner, Grace told Jon the good news about her conversation with Ruth.

"I knew something must have happened," Jon said. "I could tell by your face when I came in the door."

"How do you feel about it?" Grace asked anxiously. "Should we go ahead and have Stephen anointed?"

"What's it mean to be anointed, mom?"

"Just a minute, Stevie. Let's hear what daddy has to say first."

"I've been thinking about it, too," Jon said, "ever since they came here to see us. I guess I'm for it as much as you are. So I'm glad you called her about it."

Stephen repeated his question, "What's it mean to anoint me?"

"It's something these people do to you," Grace replied, pulling him over to her side. "They'll take a few drops of olive oil, put it on your head, and pray that God will heal you so that your hip—or your arm, or any part of you—will never get hurt again."

"Get really hurt," Jon explained. "You'll get hurt like other kids do, but it won't be serious. You won't have to miss school."

"Hey, I'd like that," Stephen said. "That'd be great. Will God do that just because these people pray for me?"

102

"Because God hears their praying," Grace hugged him tight, "and does what they ask."

"But we prayed that I'd get well when my leg was hurting," Stephen said. "And it did. Why do we have to pray again? You ought to see me—I can run faster'n Hector."

"Because God says to do it this way," Grace said. "In the Bible. And you remember that it was Doctor Price who really helped you get well last time. This means you won't need a doctor when you get hurt. You'll be like other boys; we won't need to worry about hard bumps and bangs."

"I thought you said God sent Doctor Price."

"He certainly did," Grace said. "But Doctor Price can't come the next time you need help. This means you won't need a doctor."

"Not ever again?"

"No, Stevie, we can't say that. We're talking about your bleeding. You may need a doctor for other things. Now let's read the Bible and pray so you can get to bed."

Sunday afternoon was beautiful, filled with promise. At six-thirty Norm and Ruth Swanson came.

"Did you tell Jon what I said?" Ruth asked Grace after they were seated in the car.

"I did. In fact, we read the James 5 passage together and discussed it."

"You both understand that you can't waver?"

"Yes, we do. Besides, who'd want to waver when Stephen will be totally healed."

"That's how I feel, too," Jon agreed.

"But what if he doesn't seem to be healed?" Norm asked, turning from his driving for a moment to look at them.

Grace laughed. "But he will. Whenever Jesus healed someone, that person was made completely well at that very moment. And that's the way it'll be for Stephen."

Jon tapped Norm's shoulder. "It seems to me that you're the one who's wavering when you suggest such a possibility."

Norm and Ruth said no more about the subject until they reached their destination, a rather modest house.

"This is where we meet," he said. "You get out and I'll park the car. We usually leave our cars a block or two away, so we don't draw attention to ourselves—that there's a meeting going on."

About twenty adults were seated in a living-dining room when they entered, singing softly, without hymnbooks. A man and woman checked them carefully for microdot transmitters until they were satisfied the newcomers were clean.

Ruth Swanson spoke to a man sitting near the door, and he brought in more chairs from the kitchen. Stephen sat on Grace's lap.

Testimonies were given after the singing. Then there was a time of prayer, when—to Jon and Grace's surprise—everyone prayed aloud at the same time.

Norm introduced the healing time. "Our friends Jon and Grace Stanton are here with their little boy Stephen. You remember we've prayed for Stephen before. Tonight they've brought him so that we can anoint him with oil and pray for his complete healing. 'The prayer of faith shall save the sick.'

"Jon and Grace, do you have faith that God will heal your son Stephen?"

"Yes, we do," Jon answered.

"And do you have faith, Grace?"

Grace hesitated a moment. "Yes," she said. "I'm sure God has the power to heal Stephen, and I believe what God tells us in James about bringing him to the elders of the church for anointing and prayer for healing. That's why we're here."

"Then let's proceed. Will the elders please come forward?"

The anointing was simple and the prayer brief. All the elders put their hands on Stephen's head.

"According unto your faith, be it done unto you," Norm concluded.

Afterward, during the drive home, Stephen asked, "Am I all well now?"

"Of course you are, dear," Ruth replied.

"Can I toss the hardball with Hector tomorrow at school?"

The car was filled with silence.

"I'd rather you didn't," Grace said.

"Don't forget, Grace," Ruth murmured, as they got out at home, "she who wavers— Good night, dear ones."

The following Tuesday evening Jon and Grace took Stephen to Federal Hospital.

"Why did you bring me to the hospital?" Stephen asked, as Grace helped him undress and put on his pajamas.

"So the doctors can examine you, can give you some tests. They won't hurt, at least no more than needle pricks."

"But I'm all well. You said when we went to that meeting in the house on Sunday night that I'd be all right. So why am I here in the hospital?"

Grace's voice was tense. "The doctors need to see that you're all right, Stevie. Then we can take you back home. Now jump into bed."

"I'm not afraid."

"Yes, dearest, we know—and we're glad you're not."

"Can you come and see me here in the hospital?"

"Of course, dear. I'll be here tomorrow afternoon, and daddy will stop after work. Now I think you should pray for Stephen, Jon—we must leave."

"All right. Dear Father, you know that mother and I don't want to leave our dear Stephen—and your dear Stephen—here in the hospital while we go home. But we know that you'll take care of him all through the night—"

"Visiting hours are over. All visitors must leave at once," came a voice from the speaker in the room.

"Help Stephen to be brave, help him make friends with the other children in the ward. And may we soon be able to take him home, never to leave." Jon's voice broke. "In the name of your own dear Son, Amen."

After kissing Stephen, and hugging him tightly, they left. Neither spoke on the subway ride home.

Three days later, when Grace went to the hospital, as she did each day, there was a message for her at the ward desk: "Please let Doctor Riso know that you are here, so that he can arrange to talk to you."

"How do I let Doctor Riso know I'm here?" Grace asked the nurse at the monitoring panel.

"I'll tell him."

About a half-hour later, the doctor came into Stephen's room. "Mrs. Stanton? I'm Doctor Riso. Hello, Stephen—I guess you're anxious to get back home. We can go into the consulting room down the hall, Mrs. Stanton, to talk."

When they were settled in the straight, uncomfortable chairs, the doctor began.

"As you know, we've been putting your son Stephen through a battery of tests to determine his blood picture and general condition. I'm the hematologist in charge of this testing. We found first that he has an elevated coagulation time—about fourteen minutes. His blood system does not produce sufficient fibrin. Subsequent tests have shown that this is caused by Christmas-type hemophilia. I am sorry to inform you of this, but—"

"I want to know," Grace said quietly. "I want to know everything. Don't hold anything back."

"Actually, there isn't much more to tell you. This is a genetic condition—by the way, is your father living?"

"Yes, he is."

"Has he ever had a bleeding episode?"

"Not to my knowledge."

"Well, you're a carrier, regardless. If the condition had been discovered while Stephen was still in his fetal stage, of course the fetus would have been aborted."

"Thank God it wasn't."

"Or the tests immediately after birth should have shown that he had the condition. I've been wondering how they missed both times."

"Stephen was born at home."

"At home? What physician would take such a chance as that?"

"It wasn't a physician. A midwife delivered Stephen."

"No wonder. Now, unless you have any questions, I'll fill in the release form for Stephen. You can take him home."

"I can take him home?"

"Of course. There's nothing we can do for him here—hematology no longer encompasses that treatment. In fact that's one thing we can forget about since there are no longer any hemophiliacs. It's completely unnecessary."

"Stephen's a hemophiliac?" Grace sat rigid in her chair.

"Of course. But he's probably the only one in the entire fifty-one states."

"What will happen now?"

"What do you mean—I just told you, you can take him home."

"Afterward, I mean. This isn't the end of it, is it?"

"No, it isn't. But why worry about the future? Today and every day, several hundred boys will die in accidents of various kinds. Their parents will have no warning. What good does it do to worry?"

"When will we have any further word about Stephen?"

"The medical judicial committee meets every two weeks. It may be a month until they get to Stephen's case. So enjoy, don't worry."

Grace stumbled as she left the room, but steadied herself by grasping the door frame. All the doors leading off the corridor were alike to her eyes; she was unable to find Stephen's ward. It must be somewhere—or had they already taken him to the organ factory?

In near-panic, she began to run. Then she heard the familiar voice, "Mother, here I am. You passed my door."

She turned back and entered the room from which Stephen's voice had come.

"Thank God you're here."

"What did the doctor say, mother? Can I go home?"

"Yes, dear. Right away. Or, at least, as soon as the nurse comes. The doctor is signing papers so you can leave now."

"Hooray! We'll surprise daddy when he finds me at home."

That night, after Stephen was in bed, Grace began to tell Jon what Doctor Riso had said. But she began to cry and couldn't continue.

"I don't think I can stand it," she said, holding on tightly to her husband. "Especially after Sunday night—"

"I don't either. But I guess we can stand it together. Not that I'm going to give up."

The phone rang. It was Ruth Swanson.

"Hi," she said. "What's the good word about Stephen? You said you'd probably know by tonight."

"Hello, Ruth," Jon replied. "It's bad news, the worst possible news. The doctors tested Stephen and found that his blood condition is unchanged."

"I don't believe it," Ruth said. "Either there was some mistake, or— You and Grace didn't waver, did you? Because if you did, you're like a wave of the sea and can't expect anything of God."

"Ruth, I'll have to say good-by. Grace needs me." And Jon hung up.

"Oh, Jon," Grace said, "I feel as if we're responsible for dear Stephen's condition, as if I'm responsible. I did have doubts."

Jon put his arms around her. "So did the man who came to Jesus, asking him to heal his son. Remember how Jesus said, 'Do you believe?' and he said 'Lord, I believe—help my unbelief.' And Jesus healed the boy. So Jesus doesn't demand absolute faith, regardless of what Ruth Swanson says."

THEY HAD BEEN unable to keep the fact that Stephen had been in the hospital from Grace's parents, although they wanted to.

"We're coming over," George Duncan said to Grace on the

phone the morning after Stephen's return home. "We want to see Stephen and the rest of you."

"That's just fine," Grace said, "but I'm afraid I won't be a very good hostess. I've already been crying, and the day has just begun. It seems as if I can't stop, and I'm not getting anything done."

"You just go ahead and cry, daughter. It may help you. Do you want your mother to come over?"

"No, I think not. But I'll look forward to seeing you both tonight."

The morning somehow passed for Grace. In the early afternoon she decided to visit Linda Berkowitz. It would be a brief visit, so that she could be back when Stephen came home from school.

"Grace," Linda said when she opened the door, "I'm so very glad to see you. Has something happened—something new? Come in." And she drew the other woman into her apartment, closing the door behind her.

Grace now was crying unrestrainedly. She couldn't stop.

"Here, lie on the couch. I'll make you some coffee."

Standing at the door, Grace explained her grief, "They're going to send Stephen to the organ factory."

"Oh, no. How awful." She drew Grace into her arms and, after a few moments, led her into the kitchen. "Sit here in this chair."

While Linda was making the coffee, Grace noticed for the first time that she wasn't alone with Linda. Sitting quietly in a chair by the window was a small boy. When she spoke to him, he did not answer. She noticed that his head was larger than normal.

"Linda," she said as she held a cup of coffee in her hand, "I just noticed little Price sitting there. You have so many worries of your own—I'm sorry that I've come and thrust my worries on you."

"Do you have to be always giving?" Linda asked. "Isn't it Christian to be on the receiving end sometimes—even from a person like me? I'm honored that you have come to my house to share your grief. Now drink your coffee and we'll talk."

Grace told her everything that had happened, ending with the uncertainty they faced for the next month. "But I guess Jon and I aren't really uncertain about the outcome. Oh, Linda, I could hardly bear seeing my dear Stephen go off to school this morning. I so wanted to hold him in my arms all day—hold him in my arms the next four weeks, and forever." And she began to cry again, with hard sobs.

"He'll be coming home from school soon, won't he?" Linda asked. "I'll tell you what I'm going to do—I'll take Price in to Anna Shulker next door. She'll be glad to take care of him for as long as I'm gone—she's a dear woman. Then I'll go home with you. —No, don't object, my mind is made up," as Grace tried to say something.

Anna Shulker came in to take Price, after Linda had spoken to her on the phone from another room. She beamed when she saw Grace. "My young friend, who came to my door inquiring about Linda. And you found her—or something has found her. That I should be asked to take care of my dear little boy so that Linda now can help you—it is my privilege. Come with Aunt Anna now, dear Price. And mother of Price, be away as long as you are needed. I shall care for your son with love as my own, putting him to bed if you are late. And you," she said, turning back to Grace, "wash your soul with tears. They are God's gift to make sorrow bearable."

When the two women arrived at Grace's home, Linda said, "Now go upstairs and freshen up—maybe have a bath, a tub one, soaking for a while. There's still time before Stephen comes home from school, isn't there? You can get dressed for supper, or maybe lie down for an hour. I'll promise to send Stephen up as soon as he comes home."

"Thank you," Grace said. "But if I fall asleep, wake me in enough time to make supper."

"I'm staying here and making supper tonight. Now just go on upstairs."

When Stephen came in the house, he asked, "Where's my mother? And who are you?"

"I'm Linda Berkowitz. Your mother is upstairs—I hope she's getting some sleep, because she's very tired. Do you remember

110

the doctor who took care of you when your leg was hurt?"

"Uh-huh. I liked him."

"Well, I'm his wife," Linda said, her voice breaking. "I was here in your house once before, but you were asleep."

"You were? Oh. Did you sleep here?"

"Yes I did. Now, come out in the kitchen and I'll make you a glass of milk. Maybe a cookie, if I can find them."

"They're in that jar over there." He pointed.

"Yes, I see them now." She dissolved a frozen milk cube in a glass of water. "Sit down here, eat your cookie and drink your milk, then you can go upstairs to see your mother."

After Stephen had finished his snack, Linda said, "Now your mother is tired and needs her sleep. So if she's asleep when you go into her bedroom, don't waken her. You may play in her room until she wakes up, but play quietly."

"I'll take some of my books up with me."

"Good. And I'll be making supper."

When Jon came home, Grace was still sleeping. He was surprised to find Linda in the kitchen.

"Hello, Linda. Where's Grace? Is she all right? And Stephen?"

"They're both okay, Jon. Grace is upstairs sleeping, I think, and Stephen is reading or playing—quietly, I hope—in her bedroom. I'm almost finished making supper—you can get washed up, then bring Grace and Stephen down. By then it'll be ready."

"What happened? I mean, why—"

"Why am I here? Grace came to my apartment this afternoon, deeply depressed over Stephen and what has been happening. She needed me—and do you know, it's a wonderful thing to be needed, to be able to help someone else—so I came home with her, and here I am. Now go get ready for supper. And Jon, if she begins to cry again—even with Stephen around—don't tell her that she shouldn't. Tears now may keep her from breaking later."

"I understand. Linda, you're a dear. Thank you." And he kissed her cheek.

About ten minutes later, Grace appeared in the kitchen

111

holding Stephen's hand. Jon was behind them. Grace's cheeks were flushed, but she was no longer crying. She wore a housecoat over her long nightgown.

"Hey, it smells good," Stephen said. "And I'm hungry. Let's eat." He pulled his mother into the dining room.

"What a lovely meal," Grace said, after they had finished dessert. "Thanks, Linda. Now you'll stay for a while this evening, won't you?"

"Just long enough to load the dishwasher. Then I must get home. You three go in the living room, or upstairs, and be together. I'll take care of cleaning up."

"My mother and father are coming over this evening," Grace said. "I'd like you to meet them."

"I'll look forward to meeting them—if they come before I'm finished in the kitchen."

George and Jean Duncan did come before Linda was finished.

"Do you know what this friend did for me?" Grace asked, leading them into the kitchen. "She took care of me this afternoon and then made our supper. Mother and dad, this is Linda Berkowitz. Linda, I'd like you to meet my parents, the Duncans."

"Are you that great Doctor Berkowitz's wife?" George asked. "If you are, I'm not surprised by your helping Grace here."

"Yes, I'm Price's wife. He told me a lot about all of you, so I'm glad to meet you myself. And by the way, your daughter and Jon mean a great deal to me. So anything I can do—"

"Thank you, Linda," Grace said. "You can stay for a little time, can't you? I'd like you and my parents to get better acquainted."

"I'd like to, but I'd better get home. I have a little boy staying with a neighbor," she explained to George and Jean, "and I need to get him into his own bed to go to sleep." She went to the hall closet and put on her coat.

"I'll go along with you," Jon said.

"I wouldn't hear of it. I'll be safe—" she brought a small canister of Mace out of her coat pocket, "and you should be here with Grace and her parents. But thank you anyway." She squeezed his hand, kissed Grace—who had begun to cry quietly again—and shook hands with George and Jean. "Good-by, Stephen. Thanks for being so quiet this afternoon when I asked you to, and letting your mother sleep. Good-by, everyone."

"You talk to your parents, Grace, and I'll put Stephen to bed," Jon said, after Linda had gone. "Give everyone a hug and kiss, son."

When Jon came downstairs, he went over the happenings of the past week—the visit of the FBI agent, the court order, Stephen's admission to Federal Hospital, and the confirmation of a diagnosis of hemophilia.

"Why didn't you tell us when you were going through all this?" Jean asked.

"I guess we never did decide not to tell you—it's just that everything happened very quickly, one thing followed another, and before we knew it—Stephen was back home."

Still crying, Grace said, "We didn't want to add to your own grief, and the problems you face. But things didn't happen quickly—it's been an eternity. I'd sit beside Stephen's bed in the ward at the hospital and all I could see was him lying on a cold stone slab—"

"Grace, dear, this isn't helping you any. And it's only making it harder for your mother and father. After all, you're a Christian—you can trust God for the future—Stephen's, your father's. Everything is under his control."

"I don't find any comfort in that. If only we could go back a few years, or ahead a year—and have Stephen with us, and dad too. But here we are now, with at least a week of waiting, or maybe two, before we'll hear what the committee decides about Stephen."

"And that traitor Philip Allen—Doctor Philip Allen. That only makes me feel worse about this whole thing," Jon said bitterly. "That he'll be able to continue to hold his head up in church, and quote Bible verses—after Stephen—"

"What do you mean?" Jean Duncan asked.

"He's the one who betrayed us, who put the finger on Stephen."

"How do you know?" George's voice shook.

"Linda and Price Berkowitz knew about Price taking care of Stephen, but they'd never have told. Other people in the church knew about Stephen's problem, but they didn't know that Price had helped us. That leaves Philip Allen as the only person who knew both facts, and could have told the authorities."

"Could I have a glass of water?" George Duncan asked in a voice that showed how deeply affected he was by the conversation.

"I'll get it," Jon said. "You stay here with your parents, Grace. Maybe you'd rather have coffee," he said to George.

"No, water will be fine."

The three people sat in silence, except for the soft sound of Grace's weeping, until Jon returned.

George drank the water. "Did you ever think you might be wrong about Philip Allen, Jon? There are a number of other possibilities, aren't there? Doctor Berkowitz could have told someone he trusted, or Mrs. Berkowitz could have made an unguarded remark—especially when she was so upset, at the beginning, over her husband's imprisonment. Or even you— maybe someone saw you with Doctor Berkowitz sometime, or a neighbor saw him come in here. There are all sorts of possibilities, aren't there?"

"Possibilities, yes. But there's only one sure thing, and that is that Philip Allen betrayed us. I know that's how they found out."

"Dear," Jean said, turning to her husband, "Grace should be in bed and we should be getting home."

"All right, Jean. But don't be so sure about Philip Allen, Jon."

As they drove home, George asked Jean, "Do you think I should have told them?"

"Do you think you should have?"

"I'm not sure. If it weren't for Philip Allen, I guess I wouldn't even think of telling them."

"But there is Philip Allen, and Jon's unfounded suspicion of him."

A few days later Norm Swanson phoned Jon and Grace to tell

them about healing meetings that were being held by Eldreth Rampert. "We'd like you to go with us and take Stephen," he said. "You know about the great and mighty things that are wrought through his television ministry."

"Thanks," Jon said. "I think it would be too hard on Stephen and on us. But we appreciate your thinking of us, and if we change our mind, we'll be in touch with you."

WINTER HAD settled down on Camp Meade. Or perhaps winter's winter, since the temperature suddenly plunged deeper below its usual arctic cold.

The barracks were so cold that sleeping was difficult. Men and women shared bunks, and some men and men, women and women, to conserve body heat.

Price Berkowitz continued to sleep alone. So did his friend Alyoshka (as he continued to call him), although he had exchanged bunks with the man next to Price. After Price left his work in the hospital, Alyoshka and many others—including all the blacks—began to call him Doc.

At night, kept awake by the cold and the restless sounds around them, Price and Alyoshka often talked, their voices low. Their conversations were almost always of serious matters, seldom of the light and trivial.

"How can you believe in God, Alyoshka, when he's treating you this way—keeping you here at Meade, instead of letting you be free and home with your family?"

"He's not keeping me here; Satan is. If God had his way, I'd be back home."

"But you tell me God has all the power there is. So God must be agreeing that you should be here, or else Satan or the United States government or anything else could never keep you."

"Right. But don't blame God. He has purpose in me being here, you being here."

"What kind of purpose?"

"How do I know? But he knows what he's doing. Sometimes I know too."

"If this is God's world, why is there so much evil? Why doesn't the good overpower the evil? It seems as if evil has the upper hand."

"It does, but not always. Sometime God's going to break through and clobber Satan—clobber him bad, he'll never recover. Besides, this isn't God's world—it's Satan's world right now. God lets Satan run it. But not forever."

"How about government?" Price had many questions.

"Government's under control of Satan, too."

"Don't you know that we're always to obey the government?"

"Who tells you that?"

"Some friends who are Christians. They claim that's what the Christian Bible says. I think it was Saint Peter. God put our political leaders in place, so we're to obey them."

"Paul's letter to Romans, chapter 13. Not Peter. But it doesn't say we always obey government."

"It doesn't?"

"No. Otherwise I'm not here—I'm home. Government is to reward good, punish evil, Paul says. When things get turned around—government becomes terror to good works, rewards works of evil—then we don't obey government no more. That's what this government does, so I don't obey it. God doesn't want me to. So I end up here."

"Makes sense. Do you ever worry about your family at home? I have."

"Why worry? I can't do nothing. God can. Instead of worry, I pray."

"You remember that conversation we had several weeks ago, Alyoshka? I asked you if God answers prayer, and you said yes, he does listen and answers."

"I remember, Doc."

"That night I prayed to God. I asked him to take care of my wife and little boy. And since then it seems as if I'm not worried any more."

"Now you trust. You trust God. Did you pray in Jesus' name, like I tell you?"

"No, actually I didn't. I just prayed to God, whoever he is."

"Then you don't know he hears you. You pray in Jesus' name, he promises to hear you, and answers."

"He heard me anyway. Just like a patient would come into the hospital, into the emergency room. 'Doc, this pain is killing me,' he'd say. I didn't ask who brought him, or what's his name, or does he know me already—I just went to work. I cleaned and stitched and set bones. All he needed to do was be there, with his great need. Even if he couldn't talk, he was unconscious, I went to work to help him. Or when I'd find out about someone who needed help, like a little boy who was a bleeder. Isn't God at least that compassionate? —It doesn't even seem right to ask the question."

"God has his rules. One is you come through Jesus."

"But maybe, just maybe, he answers your prayer while you're still on the way to finding Jesus. Tell me, Alyoshka, how long did it take you to find Jesus?"

"Years. It takes me years. I'm really a rebel against God, you know. He chases me, chases me, but always I dodge. I want my own way, not his way. I shake my fist at God, say 'Leave me alone, okay?' But he doesn't. He keeps after me until I can't run no more. I give in. Sweet Jesus, he catches me—no, I run into his arms to be caught."

"If God was patient with you for years, won't he be patient with me? I may have been rebellious once, may have thought there wasn't any God—you know, bright people, educated people, are that way. We don't like to admit that we need anything, anybody. Especially God. But here at Meade, I'm no longer bright. I'm no longer educated, except I do still work at thinking educated thoughts. But university, medical school, my residency in surgery—they don't count for anything when I pick up the slop pails in the morning, clean them out and put them back. I'm a pretty worthless fellow."

117

"Anybody who works with his hands instead of his brain is worthless, Doc?"

"I didn't mean that, but I'll admit it came through to you that way, so I might as well have. No, as a surgeon I worked with my hands—the same ones that clean out the slop pails. But I took credit for those hands, and for the brain that programmed them. Other people praised them. I thought I was big, important. Even when I helped people—I had sort of an inner pride that they needed me and I could do something for them. So I did—including people who weren't my patients, which is why I'm here at Meade. But now I know I'm not worth much. My hands can't do anything for anybody. And without God giving me a brain, giving me quick reflexes, giving me an education, I never could have."

"Your hands worthless now, Doc? Those hands don't pick up the slop pails some morning, we find if they're worthless. Whole camp drowns in shit."

"Alyoshka, I like the way you get down to basics."

"Most basic thing is trust Jesus. He died for your sins."

"Thanks, Alyoshka. Now let's get some sleep—and God has convinced me that I shouldn't worry about my wife and my little boy, even if you say I should. I'm sure God heard me when I prayed for them—and hears me every night. Including now." And he rolled over on the bunk, pulling the blankets more tightly around him and up over his head.

LINDA NOW CAME to see Grace every day. They spent hours together, often without conversation.

Because Grace was so depressed, because she lived with tears and could so easily have crossed the line to total withdrawal into

118

a private world, the presence of Linda was of inestimable value. Linda's gift of silence, of work alongside her suffering friend, of small talk, of touch—all these were affirmations of a loving presence and a denial of Grace's aloneness.

"Let's go shopping today, Grace, window-shopping," she'd say. Or, "Why don't you keep Stephen home from school tomorrow and we'll have a picnic in the park?" Once they visited the satellite observatory. Frequently she'd say, "Let's surprise Jon by meeting him at the subway. Then I'll go on home, and you can walk home with him."

"Why do you bother with me?" Grace asked, more than once. "I'm not worth bothering with. Here you're taking all this time to be with me, when your own son needs you."

"He's in good hands," Linda would reply. "His grandmother and Anna Shulker love him dearly, and provide a warm nest when I'm gone. I love you, and you need me—it's as simple as that."

She was with Grace when the registered letter came. After signing for it, Grace held it out to her. "Who's it from? I don't think I can read it."

Linda took the letter. "It's from the Medical Review Committee of the American Medical Association—United States Department of Health. Why don't you wait until Jon comes home to open it?"

"I can't wait. It may kill me, but I can't wait. I have to know right away. You open it and read it to me."

"It would be better if Jon were here."

"Open it."

Linda slit the envelope with a knife, then carefully withdrew the single sheet. Like the previous communication, this was a court order.

"It's to Jon and you. It's a court order to appear with your child Stephen George Stanton at the Philadelphia area thanotel on December eighteenth. Oh, Grace dear." And she enclosed the other woman in her arms.

"That's impossible," Grace replied. "There must be some mistake. Why, Stephen has nothing really wrong with him; he's at school today. We'll find out that there's a mistake, won't we? Won't we?"

119

Linda was silent for several moments. Then she spoke, "God knows, I hope so. Why don't you go upstairs and get a nap before Stephen comes home? I'll take care of making supper. Please do."

"All right, but it is a mistake. You'll see. It can't be Stephen, not our Stephen."

After Grace had gone upstairs, Linda sat for a long time. Then she went to the phone and called Jon.

"Is something wrong?" he asked, his face on the videoscreen revealing his concern.

"The letter about Stephen came, and it's bad. I thought you should know before you come home. It's a court order to appear with Stephen at the thanotel on December eighteenth."

Jon didn't say anything. But he looked as if he had difficulty breathing.

"Grace's first reaction was to deny it. There's some mistake; there's nothing really wrong with Stephen, else he wouldn't be in school. Right now she's taking a nap. I tried to get her to wait until you came home to open the letter, but she wouldn't agree."

"Thanks, Linda. I don't know what we'd do if you weren't there. What can I do? —Maybe there's nothing I can do, anyone can do. I guess we know something of how you felt when Price was sent to Alaska. At any rate, I'll come home early."

"Please do, Jon. It all makes me feel sort of futile. That isn't the right word, but you know what I mean."

"I do. Good-by, friend."

Linda turned from the phone to find Stephen entering the house.

"Hi, Linda. Where's my mother?"

"Upstairs taking a nap, Stephen. Did you have a good day at school?"

"She takes a lot more naps than she used to. And cries, too. Why, Linda?"

"Why do you take naps, Stephen?"

"I don't any more—not since I've been in real school."

"But before that."

"My mother made me. Or Ms. Beanston did, at kindergarten. I didn't want to, but she said it was good for me."

"I guess you could say I make your mother take naps because it's good for her."

"Oh. What are we having for supper—are you making it, or mother?"

"I'll be making it. And I'd better get at it right away, because your father is coming home early tonight."

"Good. Maybe he'll play ball with me. What are we going to have?"

"Let's go out in the kitchen and look in the refrigerator. Then you can help me decide. Come along now."

Jon arrived home just as Linda—with Stephen's help—was setting the table.

"Food soon," she said.

Grace didn't come down to supper. Nor would she eat anything, even when Stephen went upstairs with a glass of milk—half empty by the time he got it to her.

"I'll clean up the kitchen and then go home," Linda said.

"Please stay for a while. I'm going out to play ball with Stephen, but I'd like someone to talk to after I put him to bed."

"Well . . . I'll see."

Jon joined Stephen in the yard. They tossed a tennis ball back and forth for about a half-hour.

"Daddy, throw it harder. Don't always throw it up in the air so I have to catch it when it comes down. Throw it straight at me."

"Okay. But make sure you catch it, that the ball doesn't hit you."

"So what if it does?" Stephen said scornfully. "That's better. Here comes one straight to you."

Then Stephen wanted to throw his galactic rover around. They did, until Jon suddenly said, "Hey, it's time for you to get to bed."

"Let me try just once more to make it go round and round the way you can, daddy."

Linda was still there after Jon came downstairs from putting

121

Stephen to bed. Grace seemed to be in a heavy sleep.

"Come into the living room and sit down," he said.

"Well, I guess I can," she answered rather uncertainly. "Anna Shulker has Price, and she's already put him to bed, I'm sure. So I'll stay for a few minutes. —How's Grace?"

"I looked in on her. She seems to be sleeping."

"That's good, I think."

"Why aren't you sure?"

"Because sleep can be escape, sort of a denial of a serious problem. Not that denial's all bad—sometimes it's necessary, to enable the body and mind to regroup, to marshal their forces for the road ahead."

"What did you do before you married Price?"

"I had a master's degree in psychology, actually counseling. I was on the staff of a counseling center. I plan to go back, to start working again, in a couple of months."

"To make ends meet."

"No, or at least not primarily for that reason. The government provides me with a good pension; it's more than enough to take care of my little boy and me."

"That's crazy, isn't it? Your husband is in a penal camp, but the same government that sent him there gives you a good pension."

"It sure is crazy. But it isn't true of many other occupations. The AMA made irrevocable pensions part of the deal when they joined up with the Department of Health ten years ago."

"It still sounds like Catch-22."

"Doesn't everything?"

They were silent for a long time. The house itself was completely still; the only sounds were from an occasional jet overhead, the distant rumble of the subway, and the sounds of crickets in the garden.

Jon sensed the same feeling come over him as he had experienced the first time he met Linda, just after Price had been sent to the prison camp in Alaska. Only this time there was a subtle difference. Now he knew Linda, Grace knew her. She was a dear friend. And he was no longer her protector, her consoler;

122

she was his. Her tragedy had receded, his was front-center on the stage.

"How would you counsel me?" he asked.

"In a quite professional way," she answered. "I had better be getting home, home to Price."

"Don't go yet. I asked you a question, and you haven't answered me." He noticed how brown her eyes were. Grace's were blue.

"Yes, I have."

"What would you say to me if I were Joe Doakes and had just come in for help at the center? My physician has sent me, knowing the traumatic event I am caught up in. You are assigned to counsel me."

"Do you really want to know? I'd tell you that denial, such as your wife is experiencing, isn't particularly bad in the long run. I'd tell you that rage, even bitterness, isn't bad—it's healthy."

"Even bitterness against God?"

"Don't you think your God's big enough to take care of himself, to take some abuse from you? You're not that big that you'd scare him, even if you shook your fist in his face. But rage against the system, too—against doctors and institutions and the government."

"Okay, I'm mad as hell."

"That sounds sort of funny, coming from you."

"To be truthful, I'm not really mad any more. I was a few weeks ago, at God and at Doctor Philip Allen."

"How do you know Phil Allen?"

"Through our church."

"Why in the world were you angry with him?"

"He refused to help Stephen. He wasn't willing to get involved. Then he went and told about us at the medical center. Your husband listened, and then contacted me. He was willing to get involved, and of course paid the penalty. Maybe not for Stephen, but for others."

"I can see why you'd feel the way you do about Doctor Allen."

"But it was more than that."

"What do you mean?"

123

"Someone tipped off the authorities about Stephen. The only one who knew the whole story, including what Price did, was Philip Allen. Doctor Philip Allen, the Judas. —But I've gotten over how I felt toward him initially. I don't feel anything toward him any more."

"How do you know he did it—notified the authorities?"

"Who else? And I should think you'd be wondering who tipped them off about Price."

"Actually, the question never entered my mind. Price just sort of went public with his acts of compassion. He was that sort of guy. 'The authorities be damned.'"

"Wouldn't you like to know?"

"No, because then I'd have to cope with some feelings I'm not sure I could handle. It's better to be ignorant about some things. Now I really must go."

"You haven't told me everything yet. The counseling session isn't over."

"Well, I'd tell you not to be surprised if you or your wife went into a time of depression, even deep depression. It's another natural reaction. In fact, any emotion is natural. So don't think you have to be a passionless person, sitting up there on Mount Olympus, looking down on other mortals and their emotions. Even if you are very religious. It won't hurt if you and Grace seem to let the Christian side down for a while."

"Is that the way I come through to you?"

"Dear Jon, no. No, of course not. But there's a danger that inside yourself, buried where no one else can see—"

"Linda, you're great. That you can be so freed up to be concerned about our troubles, when you have the uncertainty of Price and little Price. I can't get over it." Impulsively he covered her hand, which rested on the arm of the couch, next to the chair where he was seated, with his own.

"Don't be too sure. You don't really know me. But if you were Joe Doakes, I'd tell you one more thing. Maybe not in our first session, but before we were finished."

"What's that?"

"You've probably had no physical relationship with your wife since the beginning of this tragic affair. You're both sort of living in your own private, suffering worlds. You can't change that now, although you should try to see things from Grace's viewpoint and enter into her needs. But when this is resolved one way or the other, hurry back together. Don't stay apart. Or else you'll ultimately be in the same boat as almost all the other couples who go through such an incident with their child: you'll divorce, or maybe, since it's Grace and you, you'll drift apart without divorcing. Now good night." She withdrew her hand from under his. "Don't bother to see me to the door. I'll phone Grace in the morning."

But she didn't. Nor did she claim her son from Anna Shulker for three days.

GEORGE BECAME withdrawn, silent, inward. He didn't talk for days, even to Jean, with whom he had always been quite open.

He felt guilty: guilty because he had passed on the genes through his daughter that produced hemophilia in his grandson; even more guilty because he had written letters that alerted the authorities to his grandson's condition.

That the first was beyond his control, and the second the unforeseen result of an act to right the government's wrong against Price Berkowitz made no difference. In George's eyes, he was to blame on both counts.

He could not bring himself to tell Jon and Grace what had happened, and so his feelings of guilt were greatly increased by Jon's bitter accusation of Philip Allen as the informer.

On this point he wasn't so sure. Perhaps Philip Allen really had alerted the authorities to Price Berkowitz's illegal medical activities. How could he, George, know that he alone was to blame for the catastrophe that had broken upon Stephen and his parents? It was certain that Price had been accused by someone, tried and sentenced, before his own letters were written to the Human Rights Commission of the UN and to Premier Zamyatin of Russia.

And so he alternated between blaming himself and suspecting Philip Allen, with the result that he did not take the first step of explaining his part in the tragic affair to Jon and Grace.

In spite of Jean's urgings, he no longer visited them. If they came to the Duncans' home, he excused himself and retreated to his study, or went to bed.

Jean suspected his reasons for isolating himself, but was unsuccessful in getting him to change.

"Just tell them what happened, George dear," she would say. "Certainly Jon and Grace won't blame you—if there's anything to forgive, they'll forgive. Don't make these remaining weeks worse for yourself and the rest of us. They're bad enough."

George didn't even acknowledge that he heard her.

What could he do, he asked himself a hundred times each day, to save Stephen's life? He seldom had thoughts of saving his own; he almost accepted the inevitability of termination. He didn't even count the days any more.

Price's suggestion that they emigrate filled his mind increasingly. Not to Russia—that was out of the question. But surely there were other places, countries that permitted treatment of congenital conditions and did not terminate the elderly.

Time was running out. He knew it, knew that he must act speedily.

Passports would take at least a week, so he would apply for them first. Then he could inquire about the country, and, passport in hand, apply for the necessary visa. Brazil sounded good to him; he knew something about it because, early in their marriage, he and Jean had provided financial support for a couple who translated the Bible for an Indian tribe near Porto Velho. But that was before the United States government, under

126

pressure from Third World nations, stopped issuing passports to missionaries.

The morning after he decided to follow this course of action, he surprised Jean at breakfast by announcing, "I'm going in to the city today. I'll take the subway, so you can have the car—if you want to visit Grace or do anything else. I won't be late getting home; I'll be in plenty of time for supper."

Suddenly the world was brighter again for Jean. She was glad she had made a small arrangement of the last flowers from her garden as a centerpiece for the breakfast table. How pretty they were.

She leaned over to kiss her husband, struggling to keep from tears. "Dearest, that will be just fine. Are you sure you don't want me to go along with you?"

"No, Jean, I don't think I do. But tell you what, why don't you invite the kids over for dinner? We haven't seen them for a while, or at least I haven't. Guess I've been a pretty poor excuse recently."

"Now don't start blaming yourself. I will invite them, and they'll be so glad you suggested it."

"Pull out all the stops on the meal. This is going to be a celebration."

She looked at him questioningly, but only said, "I will—provided they can come."

"You tell them they've got to come. Orders of George Duncan."

When he left the house, Jean waved at him from the open door, overcome with emotion at the spring in his step, the almost happy expression on his face as he returned her wave.

Something had happened. He had either closed the door on what had been bothering him, causing such deep despondency, or he had opened a door on hope, fresh hope. Whatever it was, she was deeply grateful for the change.

"Thank you, Lord," she murmured, as she closed the door against the chill of fall.

Then she called Grace on the phone.

"Mother," Grace said, her own mood affected, as she looked

into the videoscreen, "what's come over you? You actually look happy. Radiant. I haven't seen you like this since—"

"I am happy. Your father came down to breakfast this morning a different man—I think he's come out of it, out of his deep depression."

"That's wonderful, although I don't see that anything's changed."

"I don't either. But he seems to have had an infusion of hope. Whatever the reason for it, I'm deeply grateful."

"Is he there now? Can I talk to him?"

"No, he said he had some business in the city and just left a few minutes ago. But he wanted me to invite you all over for dinner. In his words," making her voice as deep as she could, "'that's an order from George Duncan.'"

"Oh, mother, I can't tell you how wonderful it is to see you acting like your old self again." Tears formed in Grace's eyes. "Of course we'll come. What time should we be there?"

"You're not going to get rid of me that easily. George took the subway and—more orders—said I should go over to see you today. So I'll be there before long. You be thinking about what you and Jon would like to eat. More orders: I'm to pull out all the stops on the meal. That being interpreted, of course, means steaks and pie with ice cream. But you can help me decide about the vegetables."

"Mother, just one thing. Linda called last night—I haven't seen her for about a week, ever since I got the word about Stephen." Her face clouded. "She asked if she could come over today. Of course I said she could. So be prepared."

"Prepared for what?"

"I have an idea she's been on a long weekend again, maybe longer than a weekend. Otherwise she'd have been in touch with me."

There was a pause in the conversation.

"Mother, what are you thinking?"

"That maybe you'd better phone her and ask if it's all right if I join the two of you. She may want to talk to you in private."

128

"I'm sure not. But I'll call her anyway. Then if she does want to be alone, I'll call you back."

"Good. Maybe I should invite her to dinner tonight, too."

"I'm not sure. Just play it by ear."

"All right, dear. I'll be there in about an hour."

Grace didn't call back.

When Jean arrived, Linda was already there. She had come only moments before.

"Grace told me you were coming, Mrs. Duncan. I was so glad."

"I thought you and Grace might want to be alone today. I could have come tomorrow or some other time. But thank you for including me."

"I've been wanting the two of you to become better acquainted," Grace said, "and this seemed like a good opportunity. You've only met once, haven't you?"

"Twice," Linda answered. "But both times were brief."

"There. So you'll have plenty of time to get to know each other today."

Jean took Linda's hand and held it for a moment. "When Grace told me that you'd be here, Linda, that only made me want to come the more. You've meant so much to her."

"Not recently, if I ever did. My life's been a mess since I last saw you, Grace. A rotten mess."

"So's mine. For several days after the notice came, the last time you were here, I just stayed in bed. Jon had all the care of Stephen, the meals to make, and everything else. I just turned my face to the wall and didn't even talk to them. Then my father went into a time of depression, and this didn't help me any. I'm only glad Jon could still cope. But even now the two of us are still sort of distant. You'd think something like Stephen would bring you together, but it doesn't. It doesn't at all."

"Can I say something?" Linda was excited.

"Please do," Grace said. "And hurry. You look like the cat that swallowed the canary."

"I just had a letter from Price!"

129

"You did! Did it come through the mail?"

"Yes and no. I've known all along that any communication with people on the outside—sending or receiving letters—was strictly forbidden. A prisoner who was released smuggled the letter out, and mailed it to me. I don't even know who he was—there was no return address on the envelope, and only this note inside." She brought a slip of paper out of her shoulder bag. "'Sorry this is such a filthy mess. I brought it out in my shoe, nailed between heel and upper. I dug out the heel. Your husband is some guy.' You know, I could hardly read Price's letter, thinking about how much I owed that poor man for the awful risk he took. He could have been sentenced to more years, if he'd been caught."

"Price is some guy. He couldn't have put it better."

"Agreed. But here's the letter. I'll let you read it."

She brought it out of her bag, unfolded it and handed it to Grace, who was sitting next to her mother on the couch. They held the closely written, thin sheet of paper, with its perforations from the nails, between them and read:

My dearest Linda,

I love you with my whole being. And I love our dear son the same.

I could stop now, because that says it all, but you will be anxious to know as much about me as I can cram on this sheet, and details of my existence during the not quite two months I've been here, even as I am anxious to know about you and Price Junior. (I've always been proud that he bears my name.) But in the absence of any word from you, I trust God and pray that you may have courage. It is now winter here, which is hardly sufficient to describe what it's like. Alyoshka calls it the white death. (Have you read Solzhenitsyn's little book A Day in the Life of Ivan Denisovich? *If not, do—there are many parallels.) Except for one brief excursion to another world, when I put on the sterile gloves again, I've been doing janitorial work here in the dormitory. (There are some euphemisms in this letter.) I'm in good shape, having dropped about fifteen kilos. It's strange, and I almost hate to admit it, but if it were not for you and Price Junior, I'd almost find this tolerable. Maybe I'm a reincarnated polar bear. The stars at night are unbelievable. (You can only be outside for several seconds: frostbite, death.) The other strange thing is that, for the first time in my life, God seems near me here. Alyoshka says, "Course he does. Made the stars, made as many of you Jews as stars or sand. What you expect?" Alyoshka is pro-Semitic, a friend. I have no other friends, but enjoy a sort of respectful relationship with a number of others—like the bearer of this letter. God keep him from being caught with it. Give Price Junior a special hug and kiss from his father. And you, dearest? Do you remember our week in the Poconos, just after I passed my boards? Until we repeat it, all my love always, and God keep you. Price. (Warm regards to J. and G. I sure hope S. is all right.)*

Grace was openly weeping as she finished the letter. "He even remembered us! Dear Price."

"He's a wonderful person," Jean said. "I pray every day that he will be released soon."

"Thank you. So do I. But without much hope, I'm afraid."

"You know, there are things I pray for without much hope, too." After a moment, Jean went on. "God doesn't say we have to have hope; he says we must have faith."

"What's the difference?"

"I'm not sure, but it seems to me that hope is an attitude toward the circumstances, while faith is an attitude toward God. When I pray, I have to have faith in God, faith that he can do what I'm asking him. But I don't have to be hopeful. The circumstances may look just as hopeless after I've prayed as before. I'm not a theologian, so I may be wrong, but this does help me to pray even when the world seems to be crashing around me and I'm totally in the dark."

"I think you're right, mother. Thanks so much for sharing Price's letter with us, Linda."

"I knew how much it'd mean to you."

"Linda, Grace and her family are coming over to our house for dinner tonight. Won't you come, too? My husband has ordered a sort of celebration feast—for what reason, I don't know. But you'd really add to the occasion, I know that. Especially if you'd let George and Jon read your husband's letter. —Not that that's the reason I'm inviting you," she hastened to add. "We all will enjoy the evening more if you're there too, with or without the letter."

"You know, I really feel like being with all of you tonight. That's super—sure I'll come. And of course I want Jon and Grace's father to read Price's letter. You're like family to me."

Jean was rummaging in her bag and brought out a square of cloth, yarn and a needle.

"What are you making, mother?"

"A crewel-work quilt. For Stephen, when he grows up and gets married."

Grace laughed, a pleased, easy laugh. "Who said you didn't have hope as well as faith?"

GEORGE LEFT the subway at the federal office complex, went upstairs and entered the huge building.

"Passports are on the nineteenth floor," the woman at the information desk said in answer to his question.

"Thank you, ma'am."

It had been several years since George had been overseas, and his passport had expired.

A few people went in and out of the office. Others waited

patiently in line for their turn. George joined the slow-moving line.

Why hadn't he renewed his passport, kept it up to date? And Jean's. So many things were clear in retrospect. But who would have thought he'd be emigrating to another country when he was seventy-five? And Jean sixty-nine.

Time was short. He thought of the time he had wasted moping around. All the good his depressed spirits had done Stephen and himself was to make the time left for processing their passports shorter. How long would it take? Knowing the bureaucracy, he was fearful of the answer. Well, the period of suspense they'd all go through would all be because of his self-pity and stupidity.

When he reached the head of the line, a gracious woman gave him the five applications he requested, and explained the procedure.

"Say my wife and I want to take our grandson on this trip. Can I get a passport for him?"

"No, the boy's parents will have to make application. Then he'll get a passport of his own, which you'll of course carry along with your wife's and yours. Or your wife and you can be on the same one."

"How long does it take to get one?"

"Oh, it's been running about a week or ten days recently. When do you want to leave?"

"Before Christmas."

"Then you'd better get your applications in as soon as possible. I can put rush on them, but it's better not to wait till the last minute, even so."

George thanked her and went down in the elevator.

On the street, he thought about what he should do next, finally deciding that it would be good to find out about Brazil's laws on congenital problems and termination. If it did indeed measure up to the necessary requirements, he could then find out about residence requirements.

He walked back into the federal office building and again approached the woman at the information desk.

"The Brazilian consulate—let's see," and she consulted a directory. "It's at Twenty-fourth Street, in the Armstrong building. You can get the subway outside and get off right there."

Back to the street and down the escalator. An express train soon came, and he sat on the edge of the seat for the short ride.

Would Jon and Grace be willing for Jean and him to take Stephen to Brazil? Would Jon possibly consider going along, and starting a new life down there? Maybe Stern International had a branch there and Jon could be transferred.

He mustn't forget about the future. He and Jean were getting older, and Stephen might need someone else to take care of him, provide a home, when he got into his teens. So unless Jon and Grace were willing to come, too—not at first, but later . . . They could finish up things here. In fact, it would be necessary for someone to settle Jean's and his own affairs, sell their house and car for them. There wouldn't be time to do all that before they had to leave.

How long did they have? He looked at his watch. Today was Friday, November tenth. Take a month, to get the passports and settle everything else—that would take them up to about December tenth. He had to act fast—that was dangerously close to Stephen's deadline. Deadline— Why had he waited so long before deciding to emigrate? He thought of the organ factory, then resolutely turned from such considerations.

"Nonproductive," he said aloud, then looked hastily around. He wouldn't want people to think he was talking to himself, like a senile old man.

At the Brazilian consulate he was referred to a young man who was, as George described him later, very courteous.

"I am Albert Gevaert. How may I assist you?"

"I have several questions, Mr. Gevaert. First, does your country have such a thing as an extended tourist visa?"

"For how long?"

"Indefinite."

"No, the longest is six months. Then you must apply for another extension, which would give you another six months.

134

But if you're interested in staying indefinitely, why not apply for a residence permit?"

"Can I do that before I leave?"

"Oh, yes. You do have independent means? That is, you're retired, probably, with a pension?"

"Yes, both a pension and a limited number of investments."

"There should be no problem. Would you be going alone?"

"No, my wife would be going, too. And perhaps my daughter and her husband would come later."

"There's a bit more red tape if someone will require employment in Brazil, but that's usually not a serious problem."

"My son-in-law's company might transfer him to their Brazil branch."

"That would doubtless solve the problem. Now here are the applications for a visa, for you and your wife. I think you'll have no trouble filling them in. Have your signatures notarized, then return here with them and your passports. That should take care of it."

"May I have a third application form? Our grandson may go down there with us."

"How old is he?"

"Six. We might keep him with us until his parents come down there to live, too."

"Here's the application. He'll have to enter on a tourist visa, but that can easily be renewed, as I explained."

"Do you have time to answer a few questions about life in Brazil?"

"Certainly. What are they?"

"First, are costs about the same as here?"

"Housing's a little more expensive, food's a little less. It sort of evens out."

"Are there many old people? Would my wife and I be able to find friends?"

"Of course. On the whole, I think our older people—if they're financially secure—tend to be a bit more, shall we say, happy, or secure, than older people in the United States. That is, if they're financially solvent."

"Do you have nursing homes?"

"No, families take care of their own elderly members. There's less government intervention, more assumption of personal responsibility. If you needed one, you could find one, though."

"I'm not worried about needing one. Are you acquainted with the way our own government acts toward people who get to be seventy-five?"

"Do you mean termination, the thanotels? Yes, I know about it. We don't do that. Somehow we seem to have more respect for age, perhaps a bit more respect for those particular individual rights."

"I've heard there are beggars in Rio—crippled people, blind people, including children. Is that so?"

"I don't really think you'd find that there, or most other places in Brazil. Maybe twenty years ago, but not today."

"Do you mean you have no blind or lame people, people—including children—with birth defects, handicaps?"

"No, I don't mean that. We have them—like many nations do. They're just not on public display. We don't all legislate our problems away as your country has done. But either their families or the government provides care."

"Including medical care?"

"Where it's necessary, yes."

"So you don't abort or kill children with physical problems.'

"The idea, to us, is unacceptable. I do not mean to criticize your own government—I realize that the United States is my host. But I have answered you openly and honestly."

"And I appreciate that. If I have any other questions, could I call you on the phone?"

"Of course. Here's my card. Good-by, Mr.—"

"Duncan. George Duncan. I think we'll like your country."

George next stopped at the Varig Airlines office on the ground floor. It seemed to him that a Brazilian carrier might be less risky than an American one, risky as far as any hassles they might run into from the United States government at the last moment.

He picked up a timetable which also contained costs.

"When do you plan to go?" the young woman asked him.

"Early in December, I think."

"Then you'd better reserve immediately, either with your travel agent or with us. Travel gets pretty heavy about four or five weeks before Christmas and New Year's."

"I hate to bother you, but do you have a big envelope I could put all this stuff in?"

"Of course. Here—is this big enough? While you're at it, take some of these folders about tours, and these about Rio de Janeiro—you'll like Rio—and Brazilia, the city Oscar Niemeyer built—and Sao Paulo. Is there room for this? It's a booklet that answers a lot of questions about our country and our people."

"Thank you."

"Here's my card, if you want to book a flight. But don't wait too long."

He walked out, with a spring in his step. He had hope for the first time in weeks. He whistled as he walked the short distance to the subway.

Just before he stepped on the escalator, he turned aside. Why go home now? Why not celebrate this wonderful new turn of events? But how, and where?

The oyster bar. That's what he'd do, he'd walk over there and have an oyster stew. He had something big to celebrate. Even though he'd waited so long to act, things looked like they were going to turn out fine. After his good conversation with the man at the Brazilian consulate, he could even hope that their passports would get processed in time for them to fly to Brazil. They still had to get these applications returned as soon as possible so their last chance couldn't escape. Mr. Gevaert was very refreshing. Not at all like most American civil service employees. He wasn't afraid to tell exactly what he thought of United States policy. George hoped the other Brazilians he and Jean would meet would be as friendly as Mr. Gevaert. He'd drink a toast to the man and his country, if he drank. But fresh oysters were the best thing he could eat to celebrate.

While he was walking the few blocks, he remembered that he'd suggested to Jean that she invite Grace and Stephen, and Jon, over for dinner.

Great, he thought. Now there was something to celebrate.

The oyster bar still looked the same as it had years ago when he worked in the city and occasionally ate lunch there. Then, he didn't worry about anything but his wife and their daughter Grace. When Grace married Jon he had still been young and the laws had still been sane. One day he had met Jon in the city and taken him to the oyster bar, enthusiastically hoping Jon would enjoy it as he had. He had found out that Jon couldn't stand oysters.

The oyster stew was better than ever. And the big, hard crackers with horseradish on them tasted great.

He hoped he could find a good oyster bar in Rio. Or Sao Paulo. How did that young woman at Varig say it? Not like sow, but rhyming with yawn. He and Jean would have a lot to learn. How long would it take them, at their age, to learn Spanish?

Or was it some other language?

He dug into the large envelope and came out with the question-answer book. "What language is spoken in Brazil?" he read. "Portuguese. Spanish-speaking people usually have no difficulty being understood."

Stephen would pick it up like a whiz. He was a bright boy. They'd have to see that he didn't forget his English.

When he arrived home about three o'clock in the afternoon, Jean wasn't there. So he had a shower and lay down for a nap. Just a short one.

Now that he had taken some action, he realized how very tired he was. He felt the weight of seventy-five years. The waves of guilt and anger and depression and fear that had washed over him during the past several weeks had weakened him, he could see now, left him exhausted—like the waves of the ocean when he was swimming on a stormy day. But the storm was almost over, the end was in sight. He could relax now.

He slept.

138

"George dear, you'd better wake up. The children are here with Stephen, and Linda Berkowitz will be coming any minute now. I invited her, too." Jean leaned over and kissed him.

"Good. I have great news for you. We're going to Brazil, and we're taking our grandson Stephen along with us. How's that for a day's work?" He pulled her down and kissed her.

"What did you say? Brazil? But that's so far away, and there's so little time left. I'd like to be as sure as you are, but—"

"You can believe me," George replied. "The time is short, of course it is—we've all wasted entirely too much of it since the problem first came to the surface. But there's enough left to make the arrangements and get down there before Stephen's date. I started the process this afternoon. Now what we have to do is wait—and attend to all the details of packing and leaving this place. It won't be easy; of course it won't."

Jean sat down in a chair beside the bed. "It doesn't have to be easy, as long as you and Stephen are saved from the thanotel. I'd even walk to Brazil for that."

"Well, you won't have to," George laughed. "We'll be going down there by a Brazilian airline."

"I can hardly believe it," Jean said, more to herself than to her husband, "that this nightmare may end without destroying us all."

George reached over and drew her to him. They were silent for a few moments, with the warm affection that was their deepest communication after all the years they had lived together. Then Jean said, "But I must go downstairs and get dinner ready, if I possibly can. I only have to grill the steaks—maybe you'll do that—but we'll wait until Linda gets here to start them. I hear someone at the door—she must be here. Now get ready in a hurry, please. Let go of me, I really have to go." There was an edge of exasperation to her voice.

He rose from the bed and shivered—not from the cold; the bedroom was warm. But his rest was not ended, his blood was slow in circulating, his mind was not completely at peace. He dressed quickly, put on a tie at the last minute, and went downstairs to the festive meal.

"Dad seems like a different person," Grace said to her mother in the kitchen while they were serving dessert.

"I know. He'll soon explain it to you. —I can hardly wait for him to tell you. In just a few hours he's come out of his depression and been almost like his old self. And Linda, too—it must be that letter from her husband."

"Yes, I'm sure it's Price's letter. But an upbeat mood like tonight affects everybody. Even me."

After dinner, Linda shared Price's letter with George and Jon. Then they discussed it.

"I have Solzhenitsyn's book at home," Jon said. "I'll dig it out, and drop it off at your place. As I recall, it's about Solzhenitsyn's own prison experience. Alyoshka is a Baptist who's also imprisoned."

"Sounds to me as if Price has run into a Christian there at the prison," George said.

"Yes, and that they're pretty good friends," Jon agreed.

"Don't bother getting the book to me, Jon," Linda said. "I've already checked, and it's in the compulibe. So I'll just access it on the videotext tomorrow. I use the service a lot, especially since Price left."

"Now tell us why you're so happy, dad." Grace turned to her father.

"How would you like to leave the old U.S.A. and emigrate to another country?"

"That's what Price suggested, wasn't it?"

"Yes—only he suggested Russia. That's out, but I've been thinking of someplace else."

"Where?" Jon asked.

"Brazil. One of the most progressive countries in South America."

"With a military dictatorship? And torture? That's not much better than Russia."

"It's not communist. And its relations with our own country are good. So it can't be compared to Russia. And if you're wanting to save Stephen's—" he broke off as he saw Stephen

140

push an automobile around the corner, from the dining room. "If you want results, you can't be too particular."

"Even if we decide it's the thing to do," Jon said, "we couldn't wind up our affairs soon enough. It would mean getting another job down there—"

"Doesn't Stern have offices in Brazil?"

"Yes, but I'm not sure I could arrange for a transfer. Even supposing I could, it would take a couple of months. And we no longer have that much time."

"I know that. So I'm proposing that Jean and I take Stephen now, and then you and Grace come later, after you've wound things up here."

"We'd still have a lot to do, in addition to waiting for a transfer, or finding a position with some other international firm."

"That's all right. You could wait for six months, if you needed to. Meanwhile, maybe we could find some job openings down there for you to explore."

"It sounds good to me," Grace said, with a tone of finality.

"Well, I'm not sure." Jon paused for a moment. "At least not yet. Maybe after I think about it. But not now. And not Brazil. As far as I'm concerned, that's just a little above Russia."

George became agitated. His voice shook as he said, "But there isn't time to think about it for very long. We have to decide soon, so we can make all the arrangements—like passports, air transportation, temporary residence visas. So there's no time to waste. There may be a dozen other countries in the world to which we could go, where Stephen would be safe and could live out a normal life. But we don't have time to track them down. A few years ago, Canada would have been ideal, but not since it started the same program of genetic control we have here. Brazil is far from perfect, but in the two important matters it's just what we're looking for, what we need so desperately: Brazil has no genetic control, and they'll give us asylum. They'll let us become residents. And they also don't terminate old people."

141

"Canada was the same, until three years ago. Then they changed," Jon said. "Who knows whether Brazil won't change, too, three years from now?"

George had no answer. No one spoke.

After several minutes, Grace put her hand on Jon's arm. "If Brazil did change, we would move to some other country."

"And become nomads? That's not good enough for any of us."

"So you'd let your own son die, you'd let them send him to the organ factory." George spoke quietly, intensely, shaking his head in disbelief.

"I didn't say that, and you know it," Jon replied heatedly. "Just because I don't go for some half-baked scheme doesn't mean I'd let my son Stephen be sent to the organ factory." He added more quietly, "If I can prevent it."

"See," George said, his voice rising, "you're not sure you can. You've already given up. Well, I haven't. In exactly four weeks Jean and I'll be flying to Brazil, and I hope Stephen will be with us. That's just one week before you're supposed to report with him—"

"Dad, let's wait to discuss this any more until I take Stephen to bed. He's been out in the kitchen, I think—he may have heard too much already." She left the room, returning with the little boy.

"Stephen, kiss grandma and grandpa goodnight. And Linda. Then up to bed."

The four people were silent until Grace returned. Then Jean spoke.

"George dear, we know how you feel. But you've got to understand how we feel, too. The whole idea of emigrating to Brazil is completely new to the rest of us—including me. You've just got to give us time to think about it, a day or two."

"You don't want to go?" George sounded shaken.

"I didn't say that. I said that none of us can come to an immediate decision about such an important matter. You've had time to think about it, to look into it. We haven't. Now you just have to give us time, too. I'm sure I'd go with you anywhere, George dear—even the whole way around the world to China. But I'm a thinking person as much as you; you can't just tell me to go and I'll immediately think it's the right thing to do. And maybe, just maybe, if you give us time, one of us will come up with some ideas or insights you haven't considered."

George quietly said, "All right. But in four weeks I'll be on that plane to Rio. Even if I'm by myself. I will not permit the government to terminate my life."

"MOM, WHAT'S the organ factory?" Stephen asked the question as soon as he arrived home from school the following Monday.

"The organ factory? First, let's get you some milk and a cookie, then we can talk about it."

"I asked Ms. Pritchard, and she said she never heard of such a place. Then later she told me to ask you. I want another cookie."

"What, Stephen?"

"I'd like some more cookies, mother. Please."

"Here you are, two cookies. But that's all before supper."

"Okay."

"What?"

"I said okay."

"What else?"

"Thanks."

"That's more like it. Now why do you want to know about the organ factory?"

"I heard daddy talk about it the other night. Is the organ factory bad? Would you send me to it?"

143

"You remember the hospital where you were for a few days, Stephen?"

"Yes. Is the organ factory like that?"

"Something like it. The doctor sends people there when they're very sick, and then they don't hurt any more."

"If they don't hurt any more, can they come home?"

Grace struggled for composure. "Usually not, I think. Now why don't you go out and play until dinner? Maybe your father will be home early, and he'll be able to spend some time with you."

"Will you send me there? Why did daddy say something about sending me there, the other night when we were at grandma and grandpa's?"

Grace was fighting back tears. "I really can't answer you. Do go out and play. Please."

"But I'm not sick. Doctor Price made me all well. So why did you talk about sending me to the organ factory? Even if I did get sick again, you could take me to the hospital. Or Doctor Price could come back and take care of me."

"I told you to go outside. Now go."

Stephen went, but he didn't play. Nor did he join the group of children playing in a neighboring yard. Instead, he sat under a tree, leaning against its trunk, tearing up some of the leaves which had fallen to the ground.

As soon as Jon turned the corner, he got up and ran to meet him.

"Daddy, why would you send me to the organ factory? I'm not sick. I asked Ms. Pritchard at school and she told me to ask mother. Mom told me about the organ factory but she got mad when I asked her why you'd send me there. Why, daddy?"

Jon looked suddenly stricken. "I'll—we'll never send you to the organ factory, Stephen." A moment after he said it, he regretted the finality of his pronouncement.

"Do you promise, daddy?"

"I make no promises on an empty stomach. Let's go in and find what mother is having for dinner."

"I want you to promise, daddy."

Jon had never seen Stephen more serious. "Some of the other kids heard me ask Ms. Pritchard, and they told me the organ factory is awful. Mom says they send people there when they're very sick, but Hector told me they're already dead. If they're already dead, why don't they put them in the ground, like Aunt Lila?"

Darn kids, Jon thought.

"If somebody's dead," he answered, speaking slowly, trying to collect his thoughts, "what difference does it make? What difference would it have made to Aunt Lila what we did with her body after she died? The real Aunt Lila, the one who visited us and read stories to you, would be with Jesus, regardless of where her body was."

"Why's the organ factory awful, then?" Stephen clutched his father's coat. "And why did you talk about sending me there the other night when we were at grandma and grandpa's, instead of sending Linda, or grandpa?"

By this time Jon had recovered enough to resume walking toward the house. "I don't know about you, but I'm hungry," he said, taking Stephen's hand. And inside the house he called, "Hi, Grace—I'm home. And we're hungry."

"Make the salad and we'll be able to eat right away."

"Good." He went into the kitchen, kissed Grace, and said in a low voice, "He tried to make me promise that we wouldn't send him to the organ factory."

"Did you?"

"Not exactly. But a minute before, he caught me completely off guard, and I told him we'd never send him. So I might as well have followed it up with the promise he asked for. I guess countdown's begun and there's nothing we can do." He dropped into a chair.

"Make the salad so we can get the meal on the table. We can talk afterward." The sharpness of her tone betrayed her consternation, perhaps also her impatience with Jon.

"Your father's proposal suddenly sounds a lot more attractive," Jon said as he separated the leaves of lettuce.

"And urgent," Grace replied. "I guess up to now I've been

telling myself it can't happen to Stephen—that there's been some mistake, that there's some way out. But when he himself begins to question . . . it's impossible to turn him aside the way I've turned my own thoughts aside."

At the table, Stephen immediately came back to the subject. "Daddy wouldn't promise me that you won't send me to the organ factory."

"Stephen," Grace said, putting down her fork, "have we ever done anything to you that we didn't think was for your good?"

After a moment's silence, Stephen replied, "I guess not."

"Then don't you think you can trust us for this, too?"

"Yes, but daddy wouldn't promise."

"Even if he wouldn't, can't you trust us?"

"Yes. Charles brought a toad to school today. And it got out of his pocket. And Ms. Pritchard didn't know it was hopping around in the back of the room—that's where Charles and I sit. And all the kids were laughing, and she made Charles take a note home. So Charles says I ought to have to take a note home, too."

"Why?"

"Oh, just because. What's for dessert?"

"Stevie, answer my question. Why did Charles think you should have had to bring a note home from your teacher?"

"Oh, because I— What's for dessert? I hope it's chocolate something."

"Stevie!" Grace's tone was sharp.

"I stepped on Charles' fingers when he was reaching out to pick up the toad. So the toad got away, and that's when Ms. Pritchard came back to see what the kids were laughing about, and the toad jumped up against her leg, and she got mad at Charles."

Grace, for several moments, had forgotten all concerns except those of a mother whose child misbehaves in school. Now her thoughts returned to the overwhelming problem, and she said in a quiet voice, "I hope you'll tell Charles you're sorry tomorrow. And it is chocolate, Stevie, but you'll have to finish your other food first."

"All right, mom," Stephen said in a relieved voice.

"What'll we do Friday on my day off?" Jon asked.

"Let's go to the shore!" Stephen was excited. "I want to get some more shells from the beach near the Coast Guard Station. And some Cape May diamonds for my rock tumbler."

"Okay. But we'll want to get an early start, so you'll have to go to bed early."

After Stephen was in bed, Jon phoned George Duncan. "First I want to apologize for getting impatient with you last night. We know you're just as upset and concerned as we are."

"That's all right, Jon."

"Then I want to ask you to go ahead on the plan for you and Jean to take Stephen with you to Brazil."

"Do you really mean it?" Jon saw George's face light up on the videoscreen.

"Yes. Grace and I have been talking, and Stephen was asking about the organ factory. He must have overheard at least part of what we were talking about the other night."

"That's a catastrophe."

"Oh, I think we handled his questions all right. But it's made us see the urgency of the situation. So please go ahead and arrange for his passport, and whatever else is necessary. We've decided he should go with you."

"I'll bring the papers over yet tonight. You or Grace will have to take care of the passport and visa. Parents have to do that. But I'll go ahead on getting the air reservations."

"Thanks, George. You'll be over before long? I could come over there for them."

"No, I'll come right away."

When George arrived, he went over the two applications with them. "You'll have to go to the federal complex downtown. State Department. The passport fee is two hundred dollars—the visa for Brazil won't cost you anything. But you can't apply for a visa until the passport comes through."

"I'll go in town to get the passport Friday. We were thinking of going to the shore, but this is more important—we should really get this out of the way as quickly as possible."

"Right. I already called the travel agency and made reservations on Varig, the Brazilian airline, for December tenth. That's one day more than a week before Stephen's supposed to report. It is December eighteenth, isn't it?"

"Yes. When will you need the money for the airline ticket?"

"Jean and I have already discussed that. We're buying the ticket for Stephen. Now don't say anything, we've decided it."

"Dear dad," Grace said. "Thank you for that, and everything else."

"Mrs. Leipert was in to see us again today. Did we tell you about her previous visit?"

"Yes. Impossible woman."

"Today she told us that at the last minute she got all nervous, and decided she couldn't drive Hugh to the thanotel. So she called a taxi. She sent her husband to the thanotel in a taxi."

"I'm glad you won't have to go, dad," Grace said, taking his hand. "You and Stephen both will be safe, and six years from now, mother, too, when she gets to be seventy-five."

"Right. It just seems to solve our problem the whole way around."

THE DAYS OF waiting became unbearable. Outwardly they were normal days, but under the surface was vague but intense anxiety that touched everyone except Stephen.

"Have you noticed that it's rained every day so far in November?" Jean asked her husband. "Such a cold rain, too. And the days are getting shorter. I can't believe that next Thursday is Thanksgiving."

"Neither can I. I sure wish those passports would come through."

"Don't worry about them. They said it would take ten days, didn't they?"

"A week or ten days. And a week has passed. I can't explain the delay," George replied.

"Have you ever known the government not to be late?" Jean asked with a little laugh.

"But we're running out of time."

"The passports will come," Jean reassured him. "How shall we celebrate Thanksgiving? Grace invited us over there."

"I guess we can't have the kids here, the way the place is torn up, with all the packing and getting ready to leave."

"No, I guess not, although— No, we'd better accept their invitation." By the way she spoke, Jean showed her regret at not being able to entertain her family this last holiday together in the United States.

"It's not going to be easy for the kids to give up Stephen for those six months or so," George said.

"No, it won't be easy. In spite of the tremendous relief they'll feel."

"And it's going to be a lot of responsibility for us—we're not as young as we once were. I hope we can cope with a lively six-year-old."

"God will give us the strength," Jean said, "I'm sure of it. I'm not worried about that—what worries me, I guess, is whether Stephen will be happy away from Grace and Jon for such a long period of time."

"If he's unhappy, we'll just have to think of what it's like at the organ factory. That will soon change the picture." George turned to leave the room.

"What are you working on now?"

"Packing my woodworking tools. I got three more empty barrels yesterday."

"What if Stephen has an injury after we get down there?" Jean asked.

"I guess we'll just have to leave that with the Lord, too. But

149

remember, it won't be illegal for a doctor to treat him."

"I wonder how Price Berkowitz is. It's been a while since we've seen Linda. In fact, we haven't seen her since she had the letter from him."

"That great Doctor Berkowitz; I'd give anything to be able to get him away from that prison camp and back with his wife. If only they could go to Brazil with us. It's not right." George's concern was shown by the force with which he spoke.

"'If only.' Those are really hopeless words, aren't they?" Jean said. "If only you weren't seventy-five, if only Stephen didn't have hemophilia, if only the government weren't so repressive, so anxious to control every part of our lives, if only—"

"I'd better get back to the packing. Will you phone the kids and tell them we'd like to take them up on their invitation for Thanksgiving? Find out what we should bring."

The following Wednesday, the day before Thanksgiving, George Duncan received a letter from the passport office. When he took it out of the envelope, a check fell to the floor.

"We regret to inform you," the printed form read, "that your passport application has been denied for the following reason." A mark had been placed next to this explanation: "Computer check of your identification indicates that:" and then this typewritten line, "Termination date within two months. Foreign travel no longer permitted." At the bottom of the letter was a note that the passport fee was being returned, and that Ms. Jean Duncan could make separate application for a passport.

George held the letter out to Jean, then sat down heavily in the nearest chair. He was unable to speak.

Jean read the letter, read it a second time, then knelt beside George's chair and took his hands in her own. She kissed them; he heard no sound of weeping, but felt her tears on his hands.

Neither spoke.

Jean shifted her position, sat down on the floor, continuing to hold George's hands in a tight embrace. They continued in silence, in the same position, for almost an hour. Then George spoke.

"Let's wait until tomorrow to tell the children," he said. "Now, how about a walk?"

The following morning, Thanksgiving day, was cold and blustery. When George and Jean arrived at their children's home, Jon met them at the door.

"Good news," he said, with a big smile, "Stern International says they'll be able to arrange a transfer for me to the office in Sao Paulo. A position is opening up in their Brazilian operations, and I can have it soon after the beginning of the year. It's not much different from my position here, and the salary will be the same. —Hey, what's the matter? I thought you'd really be glad."

"George's passport application was turned down," Jean replied.

"The computer printout on me showed my termination date. So they won't permit me to travel. It looks like I'm on a one-way street to the thanotel."

Jon was silent.

Grace and Linda came in from the kitchen, and were told what had happened. Grace put her arms around her father. Linda said, "I'm so very sorry."

Jean took her hand. "We know you are, dear. But you have so much to bear yourself."

"Come over here. Jon has a fire in the fireplace. Sit down here, facing it."

"Grace, can I help you in the kitchen?"

"No, mother. Dinner's almost ready to put on the table."

When they were seated around the table, Jon asked George to pray. After a moment's pause, he did. "Father, on this day of thanksgiving, we find it hard to thank you for what is happening to all of us. We don't understand it. But we want to thank you that you love each one of us—Stephen, and Doctor Berkowitz, and Linda, and Grace, and Jon, and Jean and me—and that you are preparing an eternal home for us, where there will be no more pain and sorrow. In Jesus' name, Amen."

"Grandpa, you didn't thank Jesus for the turkey."

"I guess I didn't. Why don't you, Stephen?"

"All right. Dear Jesus, thank you for the turkey. Amen."

George left the table.

"Where did grandpa go?"

151

"He'll be back soon, Stephen," Jean said. "Now we can eat this delicious meal your mother has prepared for us."

In a few minutes, George returned.

It was a strained time. Except for Stephen, no one ate much, and the conversation lagged.

"How is little Price?" Jean asked.

"Deteriorating. He's noticeably worse," Linda said, struggling to keep her emotions under control. "Price told me what I might expect, before he left, and it's happening. But it's still terribly hard to see it."

"And you?"

"Oh, I keep going. And I'm staying away from the Capricorn Tavern, at least most of the time. Did Grace tell you I'm thinking of going back to work? There's this newly established mental health clinic, and they've asked me to join their staff. I'm seriously considering it."

"That sounds good."

"Maybe I'll get a job, too," Grace said.

Stephen, who seemed to be absorbed in eating his pumpkin pie, said, "Who'd take care of me, if you weren't here when I came home from school?"

"Oh, I would be, Stephen. I'm not talking about right away."

"That's good, because I always want you to be here when I come home in the afternoon. Most of the other kids' mothers aren't. They work."

With difficulty, Grace said, "Stephen, you may go outside and ride your bike until I call you."

Jon spoke up. "Remember, no wheelies."

"All right. But I can really do them."

"We know you can. Now let's go into the living room."

"Yes, I'll serve our coffee in there," Grace said.

Jon stirred up the fire and put on another log, then drew a circle of chairs around the fireplace. "Here, mother and dad, sit in these comfortable chairs."

"Thanks, Jon. Have you had any word about Stephen's passport?"

"No," Jon said, "but I must confess that after what you told

152

me, I have almost no hope. After all, if they found you were scheduled for termination on December twenty-second, when they made your computer check, they'll surely find out about Stephen. I refuse to live in a world of false hope or denial."

Jean spoke quickly, "I suppose you're right. But where there's life, there's hope. —Not that I can find much more reason for hope than you can."

"Isn't there any other direction we could head?" Grace asked. "Like south, through Mexico?"

"When our government sealed off the border against wetbacks a few years back," Jon said, "they effectively sealed it off against Americans who'd like to get into Mexico, too. It's impossible to penetrate, and even if you did get in, they'd no doubt deport you. Feelings there are still pretty strong against the United States."

"How about a boat?" Linda asked, "out of New York, or Miami?"

George shook his head. "We've lost too much time. We couldn't make arrangements in the few days that remain. It'd have to be illegal, and we'd need liquid assets—which we don't have, not in the amount we'd need."

"Besides, could you get travel documents even to go to a port city?" Jon asked the question.

"I doubt it," George replied.

"A few weeks ago, Stephen found out about the organ factory," Grace said. "Actually, he heard us talking about it one night when we were over at your place. So he asked his teacher. She told him to ask us, but some of the other children heard him, and they proceeded to fill him in on what an awful place it is."

"So when I got home from work that afternoon," Jon continued, "he wanted me to promise that I'd never send him there, to the organ factory. He caught me off guard, and before I thought about it, I told him of course we'd never send him. But when he asked me to promise, I said no, I couldn't. It's put me on the spot. I've lied to him."

"God will understand," Grace said.

"I'm not worried about God. I'm worried about Stephen. What do we do when we leave him at the thanotel?"

"I'm worried about my own sanity at that point," Grace said. "How can we possibly bring ourselves to do something like that—that awful, awful thing, turning our own son over to the state to be executed."

"Not executed—thanotized," Linda corrected her, with irony in her voice. "Somehow we think we've cleaned things up, made them less obscene, when we assign a different name to them."

"Like in war, or a police action, wasting instead of killing," George said, then moved his chair farther from the fire.

"Right," Linda agreed. "But the dreadful reality is still there."

"Maybe they'd change my own date to four days earlier," George said, "so I could go in with Stephen, and be with him."

"Do you really think a government bureau would permit such a change? I don't. Too much red tape."

"I guess I don't, either."

The five people were silent, their eyes fixed on the fire. Each was alone in his inner world, alone with thoughts of the future. George broke the silence.

"Jon and Grace, I want to tell you something that may make you pretty angry with me."

"Nothing would make us angry with you, dear dad," Grace said.

"Even if you should be, I still feel that I should tell you. Otherwise I'll leave an injustice behind—by being quiet, I'll let you blame the wrong person."

"What do you mean?" Jon asked.

"I mean Philip Allen. You've been blaming him, or at least you have, Jon, as the one who informed the authorities about Stephen. Well, he didn't. I don't know who informed on Doctor Berkowitz, but I know Philip Allen didn't have anything to do with their finding out about Stephen."

"How can you be so sure?"

"Because I was the one, Jon. It was the last thing I'd have done, if I'd known I was doing it—I'd have died first. But I didn't know. I only knew that a terrible injustice had been done

154

to that great Doctor Berkowitz, and I was trying to make things right, and get him released from the prison camp in Alaska."

George then told about his letters to the Human Rights Commission of the United Nations, and to Premier Zamyatin of Russia; their failure to produce action; and the FBI agent's subsequent visit. The mail opening, the tracking down of his address.

"So you see, I set something in motion I couldn't stop. God knows I've tried to stop it, to correct my mistake, to find some way out of the awful situation I got us into, but I've failed. I hope you can forgive me. I'm sorry I've waited so long to vindicate Philip Allen."

Linda went over to George and kissed him. "You dear courageous man, endangering yourself for Price. Even if it didn't succeed, your action was beautiful."

"Yes, dad," Jon said. "I agree with Linda. You couldn't have known the result of your letters—nobody could. So there's nothing to forgive."

"Daddy dear, I forgive you," Grace said, "although you didn't do anything wrong. I'm glad you told us, though. It would have been awful to blame Doctor Allen unjustly."

The little group was silent again, lost in the mists of depression. The fire burned low, the five of them watched the embers.

"Three weeks from tonight," Jon said, "right now we'll be getting him ready so we can take him to the thanotel."

"Don't, Jon. I can't bear talking about it."

"We've got to bear it. We'll have to live with it the rest of our lives."

"Jon, would you feel better if we'd given in to Norm and Ruth, and taken Stephen to the Rampert meetings?"

"No, of course not. You know we decided that Eldreth Rampert has no special 'in' with God that's not available to the rest of us. Why should a man like that have more leverage with God than any Christian does?"

"A man like what?" Linda asked. "All I know is that he holds healing meetings, and that lots of people attend them."

"Jon's ticked off about an interview he gave a few weeks ago."

155

"Why, Jon? What did he say?"

"Well, this reporter asked Eldreth Rampert about the organ factory, and termination of seventy-five-year-olds. He sort of waffled, then said that there's nothing in the Bible to say that these things are wrong. People should get right with God, and then they'd have no problem with them."

"As my beautiful husband used to say in his honest, vulgar way, machshit. But that explains why this healer—Rampert?—is permitted to hold public meetings."

"Right. He's always stood behind what the government does, so they consider him safe. He gets all the permits he wants."

Grace rose and stirred up the fire. A shower of sparks went up the chimney. She rearranged the partially burned logs and put another on top. Its bark flared.

"I love a fire," Linda said. "There's something sort of primal about it. Perhaps we have remembrances stored deep within us of our tribal ancestors sitting around a campfire at night."

Grace spoke, "Not just to listen to the storyteller, or relive the hunt, either. For protection, too, against the wild beasts, and other hostile tribes."

"Of course. Like tonight."

"It's getting dark, isn't it. I'd better call Stephen," Grace said. "Now, don't anybody leave—it's such a comfort to have you all here with us."

"Don't worry, we won't," George answered. "I don't know what Jean and I would do without this warm group. If only that great Doctor Berkowitz—your husband, Linda—could be here with us."

Grace went out the front door, returned a few minutes later with Stephen. "I don't know how he could see to ride his bicycle, it's so dark. But he was, up and down the street."

"It's not dark. And besides, I have a headlight on my bike. Only it's getting cold. When's it going to snow?"

"Not for several weeks."

"Can I get a new sled for Christmas? The runner's loose on my old one, and it's too small anyway."

Silence.

Linda was the first to speak. "I like to sled, too, Stevie. I love the snow—so pure, and clean, and untouched by anything on earth when it first falls."

"But then it gets dirty," Stephen said. "Black and mushy and dirty. And you can't sled on it any more, or else the runners sort of catch on the dirt."

"Yes, then it gets dirty," Linda agreed. "So many things seem to start out pure and clean, like a snowfall during the night. Then they get dirty."

"But that can turn around," Grace said. "Isaiah, in the Old Testament, says that although our sins are as scarlet—maybe he meant from red dirt or something else, I don't know—they shall be as white as snow."

Linda turned from watching the fire to look up at Grace.

"That's quite a promise. But nothing could make me pure and clean and white like snow again. Nothing." She snapped her fingers.

"God can. He did me." Grace's words and her whole bearing were transparent.

"I guess I believe it's possible," Linda half agreed, "but I don't really believe it will happen to me. Like I've been praying for Price to be released before our little boy— It seems so hopeless, though. But I want you to know I'm praying for it."

"So are we," George said; "all of us."

"The trouble is," Linda said, frowning, "I veer between asking God to bring Price back home and blaming him for this mess that we're in, and that you're in, too. It's sort of like someone cuts out your heart, then you ask him to put it back in again, please, to heal it because he loves you. The God of love can't be destructive, and the power that's destructive—I don't like to call it God—can't be loving."

"I have the same problem," Jon said. "I know all the answers, but they aren't on the same level with the questions. They seem to fall short. That may surprise the rest of you, but it's how I feel."

Grace left the little circle, taking Stephen upstairs. When she returned, she explained that he was engrossed in a special children's program.

"Last Sunday Margaret Nickles—she's one of the women at

the church, Linda," Grace explained, "came up to me and said, 'I just heard about Stephen. Praise the Lord!' I just stood there. When it finally sank in, what she was saying, I felt physically ill. And I wanted to punch her. I really did. Now that I think of it, it's sort of funny I had that primal urge, to punch her, I mean."

"There are crazies everywhere," Linda said, "including synagogues and churches. You shouldn't have taken her seriously."

"But she's not one," Grace answered. "And there are other people, Christians who feel the same way."

"Then they're in orbit, too. I'll bet they wouldn't be saying— what was it she said?"

"Praise the Lord," Jon replied.

"They wouldn't be praising the Lord if it were their child."

"The strange thing," Grace said, "is that they probably would. There are some Christians who think we should thank God for everything that comes into our lives. Not just for good things, like family, and friends, and shelter, and health; but also for the bad things, like smashing your thumb with a hammer, or missing out on a promotion, or sickness. That doesn't really bother me. But they also say we should thank God for evil things, like being raped, or what happened to Price, or termination, or the organ factory, or a government that does all these things while it opposes what's good and just. That's where I draw the line."

"But isn't God supposed to be in control of everything?" Linda asked. "I'm not saying we should thank him for things like Stevie or your father or Price—that's orbiting Mars. But he ought to be able to stop things like that, or prevent them, and if he can't—"

"It's not that he can't," Jon explained, "but he doesn't. Otherwise there'd be no organ factories or prison camps."

Grace spoke, "I'm really too tired for this talk about God. All I know is that he loves Stevie and dear dad—" she reached over to take her father's hand, "and me. And you too, Linda. I just wish you'd let him take over your life. At least there'd be one positive result of all this—this absurdity."

"I wish I could," Linda said. "God knows I'd do anything to

158

bring one bit of light into this mad blackness. But I can't, not and be honest. I just come back to this, if God were really loving, his heart would break."

"God's heart did break." Grace's voice was subdued.

"I don't understand."

"When God sent his Son Jesus into the world, and we rejected him, God's heart broke," Jon explained.

"But if God's heart broke over what happened to Jesus, I'd think it would be breaking over what's going to happen to your son."

"It is breaking," Grace said. "That's one thing I'm sure of. The Old Testament tells us that 'in all our afflictions he is afflicted.'"

"'And sends the angel of his presence to save us.'" George, previously silent, finished the quotation. "Only I don't see any angels on the horizon."

"There's a war going on, a hidden war, between God and Satan," Jon said. "We can't see it, any more than Job could, in the Old Testament."

"I haven't read Job. I saw Archibald MacLeish's play, *J.B.* Price took me, when we were just getting acquainted. I'll have to read the book. I found the play very disturbing. But I interrupted you. You were saying that there's a war between God and his adversary. What are we then, helpless pawns?"

"Not pawns, but participants. Everyone's on one side or the other."

"Sometimes I feel as if I were on both sides. Or, more often, that I really am a pawn. By the way, did you see on the news about that horrible thing that happened at Cornell the other day?"

"Yes," Grace answered. "I had a nightmare afterward."

"What happened?" Jean asked.

Jon answered, "These students—six of them, three men and three women—laid out a giant chessboard on campus. Each square was about one meter each way. They painted the alternate squares bright red on the asphalt. The others of course were black. Then they got guns, and forced some students—blacks

159

and whites—to be the chess pieces. They had made signs that the students wore on strings over their shoulders so they could be read front and back: queen, knight, pawn, bishop. They set up the board with the students on their knees—human chess pieces, black and white—and then one man and one woman played a game of chess. The others, with their guns, stood on the four sides and forced the pieces to stay on the board."

"What's so bad about that?" Jean asked, with a puzzled look.

"When a piece was captured," Jon explained, "instead of removing it from the board—letting the person go—they had gotten some medieval jousting axes, and the player killed the person on the spot. It was horrible. The game turned out checkmate, and they finally killed everyone except the one king."

"What a horrible thing," Jean said, with a shudder. "It just seems as if more and more wicked things are happening every day, as if there were a triumph of evil."

"Isn't there?" Grace asked.

"I have a favor I'd like to ask of you, Jon and Grace." It was George who spoke.

"Anything we can do for you, we want to, dear dad. You know that."

"Absolutely," Jon agreed. "What is it?"

"Let me take my grandson, my only grandson Stephen, to Cape May one last time. Just the two of us. I'll understand if you say no; there are so few days left to you, and you probably won't want to give him up to me for even one day. But if you can bring yourself to this considerable sacrifice, you'll make me extremely happy."

Jean spoke. "Would I go along?"

"No, dear Jean." George laid his hand on top of hers. "Only Stephen and I. I'd like to have this one last time on earth with him, alone with him. Now like I said, don't hesitate to say no."

Grace looked at Jon, whose face showed strain. But he nodded slightly.

With a voice that she found difficult to control, Grace said, "Of course we'll let you, dad dear. When do you want to go?"

"How about tomorrow? The longer we wait, the less you'll want Stephen to be away from you for a day."

"Would tomorrow be all right, Jon?"

"Of course."

"Then I'll stop for him at about eight in the morning. That'll mean we'll be there around eleven."

"Fine," Grace agreed. "And I'll have a lunch packed and ready for you to take along. Turkey sandwiches, which I happen to know the three men in my life are extremely fond of." Grace tried to smile, but couldn't. Instead, she covered her face with her hands to conceal her tears. Jean and Linda made no move to wipe away the tears that were running down their cheeks.

"Eight o'clock, then. Tell Stephen to bring his rod along; we'll try some fishing. And dress him warmly. Those winds can be pretty fierce this late in the year. Of course, if we get too cold, we'll just go over to the cottage and turn on the heat. Maybe fry some fish, too. We'll have a big day. Now let's go home, Jean. Thanks, best daughter and son-in-law in the world, for inviting us over for Thanksgiving. And thanks for understanding about the letters. Philip Allen has enough trouble with life, without being unjustly suspected of being a traitor." He went over to the stairs and called, "Good-by, Stephen. Get your mother and dad to tell you what we're going to do tomorrow."

Then he turned to Linda, took her hands in his own, looked into her eyes. "My dear young woman, I want to tell you how much I respect you. That you can cope with the uncertainty of your husband's absence, and with your child's serious illness—such strength must come from God. And he will give you strength—God will give all of us strength—for whatever lies ahead." He leaned over and kissed her on the forehead. Linda put her arms around him and held him tightly against her. Sobbing uncontrollably, she buried her face in his chest.

After several moments, during which no one spoke, he gently drew away.

"Good-by," he said. "Have Stephen ready at eight."

Jean embraced Grace and Linda, kissed Jon, and followed her husband through the door.

161

"What a man," Linda said.

"Yes, he certainly is," Grace agreed. "I'm glad he and Stephen will have this last time at the shore together." She turned to Jon, "It is all right with you, dear, isn't it? Maybe we can do something special together."

"Of course it's all right. Now let's get at the dishes. Linda and I'll start on them, while you put Stephen to bed."

"No," Linda said, "I'll put Stephen to bed. You two work on the dishes—or better still, sit in front of the fire together. I'll do the dishes when I come down."

PROMPTLY AT eight o'clock the next morning, George Duncan pulled into the Stantons' driveway.

"Ready, Stephen?" he called, as he came into the house.

"Yes, grandpa. I have my fishing rod and the lunch. Mom made a big one. Turkey sandwiches."

"Good. We'll be plenty hungry. Now say good-by to your mother and dad, and let's get out to the car."

Jon lifted Stephen in his arms, hugged him tight and kissed him. While he was still in his father's arms, Stephen leaned over to his mother, hugged and kissed her.

"Now put me down, daddy. Grandpa and I have to leave."

"All right," Jon said, putting him on the floor again. "See you tonight."

Stephen ran out to the car and was seated, ready to go, while George kissed Grace good-by and shook Jon's hand.

"Thanks for letting me have Stephen today. And for our lunch."

162

"Hurry up, grandpa. The fish'll all be gone."

The day was cold, the sky clouded over. There was little traffic after they left Philadelphia behind and were on the New Jersey freeway south.

"Look, grandpa," Stephen said, "snowflakes! They're all over the windshield. Big ones. You'd better turn on the wiper."

George pushed the button and noticed how one blade smeared the windshield. "I knew there was one thing I forgot to do to get this car in shape for your grandmother, Stephen. I'll have to get a new blade for the windshield wiper."

"There's a charging station up ahead," Stephen said, "you can get one there. And I have to go to the bathroom."

George turned off the freeway.

"How do you pronounce E-X-X-O-N?" Stephen read the letters slowly.

"Exxon," George replied. "Same as if there was only one X. Now you wait until I tell the man what we want, and then we'll find the bathroom." He pulled up beside the attendant.

"I'd like you to replace both wiper blades. No need for a fast charge."

Soon they were back on the freeway. The three-hour drive, filled with things to see and talk about, passed quickly. By the time they reached the bridge into Cape May, the snow had stopped, although the sky was still leaden.

"We'll go to the cottage first, park the car, and then walk to the beach," George said. "Okay?"

"Okay. Only let's hurry. I want to catch some fish."

"You will," George said.

"Promise me?"

"Yes, I promise." —*Even if I have to go buy some bluefish at the wharf and put them on Stephen's hook when he's not looking,* George continued to himself.

Stephen was reminded of something. "Grandpa, I asked daddy to promise me something and he wouldn't."

"He wouldn't?" George showed his surprise. "What did you ask him?"

"That he wouldn't send me to the organ factory. The organ

factory's an awful place. The kids at school say it is. Especially Hector. He used to live near it."

"Want me to promise?"

"That nobody will send me to the organ factory?"

"Right."

"Sure I do. Wow—will you? Will you promise that nobody will never ever send me to the organ factory?"

"Yes. I promise you."

"Wow. Wait till I tell daddy. Now let's go to the breakwater. I want to start fishing."

As they reached the cottage, they could hear waves breaking on the beach a block away. "As soon as I stow this stuff, we'll head for the breakwater," George said. "It'll just take a minute. Do you want to eat our lunch here or down on the beach?"

"On the beach."

"Okay. I'll just be a minute. Do you want to use the bathroom?"

"No."

"Maybe you'd better."

"No, I don't need to."

"All right, but if you need to while we're on the beach or the breakwater, you'll have to walk back here. They've closed the men's room for the season."

"I wouldn't go there anyway. It stinks."

George soon came out again and locked the cottage door. "Now do you have your rod? I'll take the lunch and the tackle box. And the net. Let's go."

"Give me the tackle box," Stephen insisted. "I'll carry it."

George handed it to the boy, then suddenly stopped. "Hey, do you know what? We forgot to get any bait."

"You go get it and I'll wait for you at the beach."

"Okay. But don't go out on the breakwater."

"I won't. Can I have a sandwich now?"

"Sure. Here's one—look how much meat your mother put on them."

"I like turkey, but lettuce is piggy." With that he opened the sandwich, removed the leaves of lettuce and threw them on the ground. "Now you hurry up and get the bait, grandpa. I want to go out on the breakwater before all the fish are gone." Stephen started toward the beach, sandwich in one hand, rod and tackle box in the other.

George was just starting to drive away in the car when Stephen reappeared. "I can't carry all this and eat my sandwich at the same time. You take the box, grandpa."

As George drove back to the bridge, he noticed that the sky had lightened somewhat, as if to promise some afternoon sunshine.

"Fishing today?" the high school boy at the little bait shed asked. "Looks like it's going to be a beautiful day for it after all. Wish I was out there myself. Going out on a boat?"

"No, just off the breakwater. My grandson came down with me. How're they running?"

"Bluefish are pretty good. Some weakfish. How much squid do you want?"

"About half a kilo, I guess. Do you have any flounder trimmings?"

"No—but these squid should do it for you."

"They have to. I promised Stephen—my grandson—that he'd catch some fish today. And I can't disappoint him."

"I know what you mean. My father—not really my father, but my mother's second husband, the one when I was about nine years old—always used to promise me things. Then he'd never do them. Hope you catch some big ones."

George took the plastic-wrapped squid from the boy and laid a twenty-five dollar bill on the counter. "Please keep the change. And thanks."

"Hey, thanks," the boy exclaimed. "Thanks a lot."

He drove directly to the beach, parking the car on the street that followed the shoreline. Stephen ran over as his grandfather got out.

"I want to leave my jacket in the car. It's too hot."

"Why don't you keep it with you? It'll be cold out on the breakwater."

"No, it's warm."

165

"It doesn't really seem warm to me, Stephen. . . . But, all right, put it inside for now. Where are your shoes?"

"Down on the beach. On the rocks. The sand's nice and warm."

"Well, leave your sweater on. I can't have you catching cold."

"I won't catch cold. Come on, grandpa." And Stephen ran down to the sand. "See, the tide's out—there's lots and lots of sand. And shells, only they're all these same old clamshells. Can we go up by the Coast Guard beach and hunt for shells there? They've got nice ones."

"Later this afternoon. Now let's eat this lunch and get out on the breakwater, so we can begin to fish."

"Let's eat out on the breakwater." And Stephen was already heading across the sand for the automobile-size boulders that tumbled out into the ocean in a straight line. George remembered hearing how they'd been excavated at building sites in Manhattan and brought down by barge.

"Hey, Stephen, slow down!" George called. "Careful you don't fall—wait for me."

Stephen slowed his pace a bit, but still went from boulder to boulder without stopping until he reached the end of the breakwater.

"I beat you," he said, waving his fishing rod. "I got here first."

George clambered over the rocks, a bit unsteady, as he carried his own rod, tacklebox, collapsible landing net, package of bait and lunch box.

"There's a smooth rock you can sit on, grandpa. And you can lean back against that other one."

"I'd have to lean too far back. I think I'll sit on this one. Now let's eat. Will you pray, Stephen, and thank the Lord for the lunch your mother packed?"

"No, grandpa. You pray."

George simply said, "Thank you, God, for this beautiful day, this good food, and that Stephen and I can be together. Amen. —Here's another turkey sandwich, Stephen. And this big apple."

"I don't want any apple. Can't we use it for bait? Or I could throw it out on the water and maybe it would float across to some other place."

George did not reply.

Fall and winter, spring and summer: he remembered the breakwater and its surrounding beach in all the seasons. That first time, when he was a young boy—could he have been Stephen's age?—and he had gotten so badly sunburned. He remembered how concerned his mother was that she hadn't watched him more closely. And how he'd worried a week later when his skin peeled from the burn, that the rough edges would never heal. Stephen wouldn't get a chance to have those little worries.

He remembered other happy days on this beach when Grace was a little girl, building sand castles, riding the waves in to shore, running back out with Grace perched on his shoulders. How Jean had liked to read, lying on a beach towel.

"I said I'm finished with my lunch, grandpa. Help me put some bait on my hook."

George produced a penknife from his pocket, cut off a piece of the squid and handed it to Stephen. "You'll have to bait your own hook. And clean your own catch."

"I can't clean the fish. My daddy does it for me."

"Well, you'll clean them today. Otherwise no fish for you for supper."

"Are we staying down for supper?"

"Yes. We'll go back to the cottage late in the afternoon. Then we'll clean our fish and fry them."

"On line! Now please bait my hook."

"I said you were going to bait your own hook. Put the squid on like this." And he slowly showed the boy how to do it, baiting his own hook. "It's simple."

"I know it is, but I hate the squishy feel, and putting the hook through." While Stephen talked, he haltingly baited the hook. "It's worse with worms or tadpoles, though. Now I'm ready."

"Cast it out real far. That way it won't get snagged so easily on the rocks."

The water was gray-green, almost black. George watched the

167

waves begin their buildup a little farther toward shore than where Stephen and he stood on the breakwater, gather momentum, and then crash on the beach. Beyond the beach a row of Victorian houses, boarded up for the winter, lined the road.

He turned back toward the ocean. On the horizon an oil tanker passed, moving almost imperceptibly. How he would love to be on that ship with Stephen, going to another country.

"Look at the ship," he said to Stephen.

"I see it. And there's a fishing boat—I wonder if they're catching anything."

The old man and the little boy fished in silence for almost an hour. Twice George had to free his grandson's line, once he had to unsnarl it.

"Grandpa, I've got a bite!"

"Jerk the rod just a little to set the hook. Now don't start reeling it in fast. Let him have some line—don't be in too much of a hurry. We have all afternoon. Looks like you have a big one."

"I do, a huge one. Help me hold the rod."

"You're strong enough to bring him in yourself. Don't step off the end of the rocks there—I don't want to have to fish you out of the water."

Stephen finally brought the fish near enough for the old man to catch it in his landing net.

"Looks like a bluefish. And a big one. Must weigh about two kilos. He's a beauty. Now I'll hold him while you take the hook out of his mouth. There."

Stephen took the fish from his grandfather and held it aloft. When it suddenly jerked with a wild spasm, he dropped it on the rocks. George quickly recovered the fish and put the stringer through its gill and mouth.

"You've got to be careful or you'll lose a fish that way," he warned Stephen.

"You caught it so it didn't get away, grandpa."

"Yes, but I might not have been there. Or been quick enough. Now we'll put this fish back in the water and attach the cord around this rock—I mean, we'll roll this rock onto the cord. Then he'll be safe."

168

"I'm hungry."

"Here's the lunch. There are two sandwiches left—one's peanut butter, I think. And there are some cookies, and more fruit. Take what you want."

"All right. I'm glad I don't have to eat squid, like fish do."

"You'd prefer it to peanut butter, if you were a fish."

"But I'm not."

Several gulls circled overhead, screeching loudly.

The old man and the boy fished for two more hours, but they caught nothing except for a baby shark that George landed.

"He's ugly," Stephen said. "Ugh—throw him back in. Let's go back to the house. I'm tired of fishing." He took hold of the stringer and brought the bluefish up out of the water. "I'll carry my fish."

They picked up all the gear and the plastic coverings of the lunch, then retraced their steps to the beach. The sun was getting low on the horizon and the wind had increased.

"I'm cold. I want my jacket."

Back at the cottage, George said, "Go around to the back and put the fish on the picnic table. I'll get a big knife and a pan of water." He went into the house, soon returned.

"Here's the knife," he said. "First cut off the head—here, bear down harder." He put his hand over the little boy's. "That's right. Now cut off the fins and the tail. Farther back. Now make a slit along the bottom, under the belly—deeper, it has to open up. That's right. Now reach in and pull everything out that's loose."

"What's this, grandpa?"

"The liver. Now put all that gook down on this plastic and we'll wrap it up. Right. Now you've got to get all the scales off—start at the back and work forward. Go against the scales. Rinse your knife off in the water."

"I got some in my mouth."

"Well, spit them out. —Hey, not on me. Now you're just about finished. Give me the knife and I'll fillet it and take the bones out. Won't that taste good? Nothing better than bluefish. Now rinse these two pieces off in the water—that's the way— and throw the water out on the dead flowers over there. You did a good job, cleaning the fish. Shall we go in the house and find what else we have for supper? I'm glad we didn't close the cottage up earlier this fall."

"Grandpa, let's go to the Coast Guard beach first. It'll be too dark to find any shells if we wait till after we eat."

"Fine. I'll just put these fillets inside the cottage, and turn up the thermostat so it's warm when we get back. Then we can go."

"Okay, grandpa. I hope we find some of those big shells there."

"Maybe we will. Let's go in the car—otherwise, if we walk, it'll be dark by the time we get there."

At the beach Stephen found a number of different shells, which he put in the trunk of the car.

"Look at this big one," he said. "I'm going to take it to school with me, to show Ms. Pritchard and the other kids."

"Now we'd better head back to the cottage again," George said. And after they got out of the car, "Have you enjoyed today?"

"Sure, grandpa. Especially catching my very own fish. Wait till I tell mom and dad about my fish. How big was it, again?"

"This big," George replied, indicating a distance of about forty centimeters between his outstretched hands.

They went into the house.

"It's still cold in here."

"I know. I'll turn the thermostat up a bit more and it'll soon be warm. Let's see what we have on the shelves here: baked beans, green beans, spaghetti, instant milk, soup—"

"I want baked beans with my fish. And that's all. Except some milk and some bread with jelly."

"All right. I'll have to see if there's any bread in the freezer. Yes, there is. Now you find something to do while I make supper for us."

"I wish we had computer TV here," Stephen said.

"That's the best thing about this place, that we don't. The toy box is in the bathroom closet—you can get it out."

"Okay. Make plenty of beans, grandpa. I'm really hungry."

"I will." George washed the fish in the sink, dredged it in flour, and heated cooking oil in the frying pan. He called to

Stephen, "This bluefish is going to taste great. And you caught it."

The smell of frying fish soon filled the cottage, along with coffee that George boiled in a pan.

Before long, the meal was ready. George and Stephen sat at the kitchen table to eat it.

"My fish tastes good, doesn't it?" Stephen asked.

"Sure does. And it's a big one. I think God brought that fish right up to your hook."

"Can God do something like that?"

"Of course he can. Do you remember how Jesus told his disciples where to throw their nets out of the boat when they were fishing and hadn't caught anything? They followed his directions, and caught a big load of fish just like that."

"God can do anything, can't he?"

"He sure can. Now let's get things cleaned up so we can go back down to the beach."

"Can we just sit there and watch the waves before we go home?"

"Of course. And the stars. Let's take this blanket to sit on. Are you going to be warm enough?"

"Sure, grandpa. I'm wearing my jacket, and I've got a sweater on under it."

"I'll bring a coat along for you, just in case."

When they reached the deserted beach, George spread the blanket out on the sand.

"Now let's sit down on it. Or if you want to, you may lie down."

"Look at the stars, grandpa. And there's a ship out there, I can see its lights. It hardly seems to be moving. I like to be here on the beach. It's so quiet."

"I do, too."

"Where do you think the big ship's going to?"

"It's headed south. Maybe to South America. That's where I wanted to go."

"Why, grandpa? And why couldn't you? Wouldn't grandma let you?"

"I just thought we'd be happier there. And no, grandma

171

wanted to go, too—but the government wouldn't let us."

George was silent. His eyes were fastened on the moon, just appearing above the horizon. Waves broke on the beach. The tide was coming in.

"We'll have to move the blanket soon, grandpa, or it'll get wet."

"Will it? Stephen, have you ever thought of heaven?"

"Heaven is where Jesus is."

"Yes, and in heaven there's no more sickness, or sadness, or crying."

"I don't cry. I'm big now."

"I'm sure you are, Stephen. Have you ever thought of going to heaven, of going to be with Jesus?"

"No. I want to stay with mother and daddy. If they went to heaven, I'd want to go too."

"Maybe you'd go first, and they'd follow you."

"How would you go?"

"You could walk there from here, right from this beach."

"Would you walk with me?"

"Yes, I would."

"Could I take my big shell?" He picked it up.

"Of course. Only there'd be bigger shells than that in heaven, and streets of gold, and beautiful jewels, and a river that's pure water—it's not polluted. And angels, and Jesus."

"Jesus?"

"Yes. He'd come to meet you."

"I wouldn't want to go alone. Especially at night."

"You wouldn't have to. I'd go with you, right at your side. Or I'd carry you. And soon it wouldn't be night any longer."

"Are we going home soon, grandpa?"

"Wouldn't you like to go to heaven?"

"Maybe. If you went with me."

"Here, put on this coat." George put Stephen's arms through the sleeves of a heavy woolen coat—one of his own, an old one, that he kept at the cottage. The little boy was lost in it; the coat dragged on the ground.

"Now see that silver path?" He pointed to the shimmering

track of light that came from the full moon across the waves. "That's the path to heaven."

"It'll be cold, and we'll get wet."

"Your sweater and jacket, and my coat will keep you warm. And soon you won't feel the cold or wet. Here, take my hand."

The boy's small hand was enclosed in the old man's thin one. They walked down the beach to the water. A wave broke over their legs.

"It's cold. And wet."

"It won't be, soon. We'll be with Jesus."

They kept walking into the ocean, the old man and the little boy.

"Let's sing." George began in a faltering voice that became more steady, "'Jesus loves me, this I know, for the Bible tells me so.'"

"I can hardly hear you, grandpa. The waves are too loud. Carry me, please."

"Sure, dear Stephen." And reaching down, he lifted the little boy—now crying—into his arms.

"'Little ones to him belong.'" A wave broke over their heads. "'They are weak, but he is strong. Yes, Jesus loves me. Yes, Jesus loves me. Yes, Jesus—'"

"Pray ye that your flight be not in the winter."

—JESUS, Matthew 24:20